The Slaughter of God

The Slaughter of God

Theologies from Jonestown

Jeff Hood

RESOURCE *Publications* • Eugene, Oregon

THE SLAUGHTER OF GOD

Copyright © 2016 Jeff Hood. All rights reserved. Except for brief quotations in critical publications or reviews, no part of this book may be reproduced in any manner without prior written permission from the publisher. Write: Permissions, Wipf and Stock Publishers, 199 W. 8th Ave., Suite 3, Eugene, OR 97401.

Resource Publications
An Imprint of Wipf and Stock Publishers
199 W. 8th Ave., Suite 3
Eugene, OR 97401

www.wipfandstock.com

PAPERBACK ISBN: 978-1-5326-3386-7
HARDCOVER ISBN: 978-1-5326-3388-1
EBOOK ISBN: 978-1-5326-3387-4

Manufactured in the U.S.A.   JUNE 28, 2017

For The Slaughtered

Contents

* These are the ordered words of the Jonestown theologies. Discover their meaning and live their truth.

Preface | xiii
The Beginning | 1
   Tried | 3
   Lies | 4
   Lay | 6
   Violence | 8
   Threats | 10
   Suicide | 11
   Worked | 13
   Lied | 15
   Revolutionary | 17
   Back | 18
   They | 19
   Dissent | 21
   Interruption | 23
   Late | 24
   Control | 26
   Lot | 28

Contents

For | 30
Hope | 32
Agitation | 34
Hell | 36
Belief | 38
Fearful | 40
Never | 42
Worth | 44
Similar | 46
Fly | 48
Value | 50
Hope | 52
Someday | 54
Choose | 56
Tired | 57
Applauding | 59
Meaning | 61
Friend | 62
Troubles | 64
Late | 65
Revolution | 67
Prophet | 69
Afraid | 71
Babies | 73
Peace | 75
We | 76
Flattery | 78
Fool | 80
Infamy | 82

Contents

Destruction | 83
Beautiful | 85
Down | 86
Incarnate | 88
Separate | 90
Choose | 92
Leave | 94
Extended | 96
Regret | 98
Season | 100
Scared | 102
Rebuke | 104
Burdens | 106
Fire | 110
Take | 113
Ready | 114
Sovereign | 116
Protest | 117
White | 118
Accept | 120
Endangered | 121
Hostile | 123
Run | 125
All | 127
Now | 128
Please | 130
Respect | 131
Sit | 132
Tried | 134

Contents

Felt | 136
Broke | 137
Heart | 138
Over | 140
Legacy | 142
Medication | 144
Afraid | 146
Good | 148
Provoked | 150
Blame | 152
Appreciation | 154
Only | 155
Hasten | 157
Move | 159
Calm | 161
Crying | 162
Therapist | 164
Rest | 166
Feels | 167
Crying | 169
Misbelief | 171
Abusive | 173
Pushing | 175
Revolutionary | 177
Pay | 178
Humane | 180
Relax | 182
Dad | 184
Friend | 186

Contents

Separate | 188
Dignity | 190
Mother | 192
Free | 194
Quiet | 196
Annihilation | 198
Quickly | 200
Laying | 202
Want | 204
Parents | 205
Tears | 206
Drink | 208
Loving | 209
Vat | 211
On | 213
Complicit | 215
Sing | 217
Relaxation | 219
Protesting | 221
Conclusion | 223

Preface

IN THE MIDST OF great evil, God is never lost. I have long wondered how Jonestown fits into the continual presence of God. In the 1970s, Jim Jones and the Peoples Temple founded a settlement in the jungles of Guyana. After a few years of communal living, Jones led his followers to commit a mass suicide/murder that left over 900 people dead. The last words the community ever heard were recorded. Jones' words are beyond disturbing. Evil resonates with every syllable. Even in the midst of the terror, I refused to believe that God was absent. Knowing that God is found in times of death, I've decided to seek the divine in the last words Jonestown ever heard. In these words of death, may there be something for us. This is not about Jim Jones. This is a search for God.

I was 12.

Everyone was asleep. The darkness ushered in all sorts of fears. Every so often, I heard something. Maybe I didn't? Was it the end or just the beginning? I wondered what was behind that old wooden wall. The documentary filled my eyes. I couldn't turn away. The people sang and danced with no idea of what was coming. Did I see something in the window? Was someone whispering? The shots rang out. Body after body collapsed. Blood poured onto the runway. Could I watch the rest? I was starting to think that I'd already watched more than I could handle.

Despite my fears, I simply couldn't turn away. I could feel the weight increasing on my chest. Then, Jim Jones started to speak. Extolling the virtues of suicide, Jones convinced the community to

PREFACE

die. I could hear the cries. I could see the vat. I could feel body after body collapsing. I've experienced it over and over. The documentary ended with images of bodies strewn throughout Jonestown. Death reigned. Something tapped against the window. I jumped. It was only a bug. For weeks, I tried to think about something else. I couldn't. I was stuck. In the almost 20 years since, I've never been able to leave. Jonestown is a part of me and I'm a part of Jonestown.

As death approached, God was there. I'm convinced of it. How could God not have been? People were dying. People were in pain. People were scared. These are the spaces where God lives. No matter how deadly, God was there. No matter how painful, God was there. No matter how scary, God was there. In fact, the God that was in Jonestown is more God than God. In this book, I have set out to know the Jonestown God. In my journey, the immortal prophets of Jonestown have guided me. Step by step, they walked me through the redemption process. When we arrived at the settlement, the bodies gave me salvation. I touched them and they touched me. I am forever changed. The Jonestown God is still speaking. Open your heart and you will hear them too.

In Jonestown, no public meeting went unrecorded. So, when the community gathered to die . . . the recorder was there. The last tape was it's finest. In the midst of the chaos, the recorder didn't flinch. No word was missed. The "Death Tape" was the result. This work is based on the FBI's transcription, Q042. Join me, as I search for God in the words of the recorder.

Jeff Hood
May 9, 2017

The Beginning

Jim Jones: I have loved you . . .

Tried

"... *how very much I've tried my best to give you the good life.*"

—JIM JONES

I'VE HEARD THIS TYPE of language my whole life. Such assurances are about the speaker not the hearer. Those who utter such words do so in order to gain control. They expect a certain response. The good life is lived not given. I can't imagine God ever using Jones' words. Love is a choice not a demand. The people of Jonestown moved to Guyana in search of something more. When the dreams became a nightmare, Jones wanted to feel the control one last time. The people were just desperate for life. So are we.

Amen.

Lies

"In spite of all that I've tried, a handful of our people, with their lies, have made our lives impossible."

—JIM JONES

The quickest way to control people is to create a common enemy. Once fear of impending consequences is established, people will do whatever they're told. There is no clearer modern example of this than Jonestown. In the midst of a manufactured paranoia, Jim Jones led the community to death. The people followed because they didn't believe they had a choice. They believed life was impossible. It wasn't. God has never been about impossible. Neither should we be.

Amen.

Jim Jones: There's no way to detach ourselves from what's happened today. Not only–We're in a compound situation, not only are there those who have left and committed the betrayal of the century, some have stolen children from others and then seek right now to kill them because they stole their children, and we are sitting here waiting on a powder keg. I don't think it is what we want to do with our babies. I don't think that's what we had in mind to do with our babies. It was said by the greatest of prophets, from time immemorial . . .

Lay

"No man may take my life from me; I lay my life down."

—JIM JONES

IN A PARAPHRASE OF John 10:18, Jim Jones uses the words of Jesus to try to convince the community of the virtues of suicide. The problem with such a connection is that Jesus laid down his life for others. Jones was seeking to convince people to lay down their lives for/with him. While he doesn't explicitly say this, Jones knew that his days were numbered due to a variety of health issues and he didn't want to die alone. I believe that Jones' fear is what caused the entire tragedy. He was out of control. When Jesus said these words, he was in control. If we are to give our lives, we must have our lives to give. Jesus gave what he had. Jones didn't. He was trying to take life. The tragedy of Jonestown is that the people had already given their lives away. When the suicide came, there was nothing left. There was no way to resist. Hold tight to that which is only yours to give.

Amen.

Jonestown Crowd: Yeah!

Jim Jones: So, to sit here and wait for the catastrophe that's going to happen on that airplane (it's gonna be a catastrophe)... Almost happened here, almost happened, the congressman was nearly killed here... But you can't steal people's children.

Violence

"You can't take off with people's children without expecting a violent reaction."

—JIM JONES

THE CHILDREN OF JONESTOWN were raised communally. Everyone had responsibility for each of them. They were "our" children. Because of the structure, the children were communally owned. Since Jonestown was built on the idea that the children would eventually carry on the community's ideals, the residents had no ability to deal with children leaving. It felt like the future was leaving. I believe this is one of the reasons the community reacted so violently. Children are never owned. The people of Jonestown forgot that. Children are the future. There is no future when children are enslaved to the constructed ideals of the present. Children must be free to engage the future. If children are not free . . . you can expect violence.

Amen.

Jim Jones: And, that's not so unfamiliar to us, either, even if we were Judeo-Christian, even if we weren't Communists.

Threats

"The worldly kingdom suffers violence and the violence is triggered by force."

—JIM JONES

USING THE WORDS OF Jesus, Jones sought to convince his people that outside violence surrounded them. Jones used real or imagined threats to control Jonestown. In the final hours, Jones repeatedly told them they were victims. He left out the massacre that some had just perpetuated. Regardless, Jones was the ultimate perpetuator of violence. Constantly, Jones divided and destroyed. That is not to say that outside forces didn't direct violence toward the community. It is important to remember that violence is always evil. Violence is always a futile pursuit. In Jonestown we see the forgone futile conclusion, violence births violence until there is no one left to perpetuate violence. The mass suicide/killing at Jonestown was a result of an addiction to violence . . . violence against the other and violence against the self. Violence was created until violence was finished. While there are many lessons from Jonestown that are very complex, one is not. If we are to experience any wholeness in this life, we must kill violence before violence kills us.

Amen.

Suicide

"If we can't live in peace then we must die in peace."

—JIM JONES

I'VE STUDIED ACTIVISTIC SUICIDES for a number of years. In every case, the idea that one can give their life to bring about justice draws the participant to the act. The concept is not without precedence. Since he had knowledge of what was coming, I would argue that Jesus committed an activistic suicide. Throughout time, people have given their lives seeking to bring about change. Most of the time, the intended result doesn't match the actual outcome. Under increasing pressure, Jones thought that a mass activistic suicide would be an example of what it means to experience peace after dying for justice. The problem is that most people were horrified by the act and never considered that there could be anything just or peaceful about it. Though I doubt it, perhaps Jones' intention was for the community to simply die in peace. If so, I hope they found it. Since God's love knows no boundary, I bet they did.

Amen.

Crowd: Applause

Jim Jones: We've been so betrayed, we have been so terribly betrayed, but we've tried, and . . .

Worked

"... *as Jack Beam often said (and I don't know where he's at right this moment, poor Jack), he says if it's only worked one day, it was worthwhile...*"

—JIM JONES

In Jonestown, Jack Beam served the community as an engineer. By all accounts, Beam was a generous and loving person. In the hour of death, Jim Jones shared a quote from Beam to push the people forward. Just because Jones used Beam's quote for evil doesn't make it evil. When he previously shared the quote, Beam was seeking to encourage people. What did he think when he heard the quote for the last time? For many that lived there, Jonestown was a success for at least a day. So was it worthwhile? For many, it was. The end doesn't determine whether it was. The days do. There were many residents who were boldly following God and seeking community. Isn't that what we're all supposed to do? While I'd encourage everyone to chase the days that work... I'd also encourage you to carry caution along the way.

Amen.

Crowd: Cheers

Jones: Of what's going to happen here in a matter of a few minutes, is that one of the few on that plane is gonna shoot the pilot. I know that. I didn't plan it, but I know it's gonna happen. They're gonna shoot that pilot, and down comes that plane into the jungle and we had better not have any of our children left when it's over, 'cause they'll parachute in here on us. I'm telling you just as plain as I know how to tell you, . . .

Lied

"... I've never lied to you ... I never have lied to you."

—JIM JONES

WHEN SOMEONE TELLS YOU they've never lied to you, they're usually lying. We now know that Jim Jones consistently lied. Lies were utilized to maintain control. Those who build communities based on truth don't have to lie. I've often wondered what Jonestown would have been like if it wasn't based on lies. Imagine a loving people working as one. Perhaps, on some days this is the way it was. According to those who survived, on most days it wasn't. Regardless, truth must hold any community together. Lies destroy such things. God is truth. God is future. A departure from the truth is a departure from future. The absence of truth caused the deaths at Jonestown. Despite the lies, God was there when the bodies started to collapse. Truth never leaves.

Amen.

Jim Jones: *I know that's what's gonna happen, that's what he intends to do and he will do it. He'll do it. What's there being so bewildered with many, many pressures on my brain, seeing all these people behave so treasonous, it is just too much for me to put together, but, I now know what he was telling me and it'll happen. If the plane gets in the air even. So my opinion is that we . . .*

Revolutionary

"... be kind to children and be kind to seniors and take the potion ... and step over quietly because we are not committing suicide. It's a revolutionary act."

-JIM JONES

WHEN JIM JONES SET the mechanism of mass suicide into motion, most didn't need to be convinced. They'd already given their lives. Some did. Jones manipulated all with talk of revolutionary suicide. What does the phrase mean? Did Jesus commit revolutionary suicide? Didn't he know what was coming? Jesus never offered resistance. Eventually, the result is exactly what Jesus chose ... death. Anyone who makes a willing decision to die with full knowledge of what they're doing ... commits suicide. Out of deep love, Jesus committed revolutionary suicide. The difference between Jonestown and Jesus is the agency of the participants. Hundreds of children could not have consented to suicide. There were so many others incapable of consent. Death without consent is murder. Many were forced. Revolutionary suicide is chosen not coerced. Jesus calls us to revolution ... not extermination.

Amen.

Back

"We can't go back."

—JIM JONES

CAN WE GO BACK? It's a timeless existential question that has consistently troubled the human mind. You can't convince a people to destroy their bodies without convincing them that there's no path back to life. Suicide is a decision devoid of a future. One would think that any spiritual leader would seek to offer hopeful words in such a dark moment. Not Jones. His primary interest was death. Honestly, it couldn't come fast enough for him. Before the day was over, bodies littered their compound. It didn't have to go down like this. With a hopeful word, the people could have been saved. Alas, it was not to be. Know . . . you can always go back. Redemption will find you there. The past is no match for Jesus.

Amen.

They

"They won't leave us alone."

—JIM JONES

THEY. IT'S AN ODD word. The four combined letters are only needed because US has failed. You see, the distance between peoples is always THEY. THEY sneaks up into the fabric of our lives and the next thing you know everyone is THEY. The further we slip and hide, the more we THEY the world. When these words were spoken, death was near. Jones planned it that way. To complete the task, Jones reverted to a reliable word. This wasn't the first time the words had been slung around. Constantly, Jones had talked about the evil of the THEY. On the last night, THEY were closing in. Jones wanted to make sure everyone was scared enough of THEY to stick together until they were all dead. We must be cautious of THEY. THEY have a way of isolating and destroying US.

Amen.

Jim Jones: They're now going back to tell more lies which means more congressmen. And there's no way, no way we can survive. Anybody...

Dissent

"Anyone that has any dissenting opinion, please speak..."
—JIM JONES

THE END WAS RAPIDLY approaching. In the midst of the slow march toward death, Jim Jones wanted to know if anyone had a dissenting opinion. Though this is a curious moment, it's not completely unexpected. Throughout history, leaders have asked for dissent for the sake of appearing like they're open to dissent. No matter what anyone would have said in those final hours, Jones was determined to make sure that nobody made it out alive. Such a moment reminds me of Jesus' advice to be "wise as a snake." There was a snake loose in Jonestown. There will be more. Don't forget, the snake can't be avoided unless you think like a snake.

Amen.

Jim Jones: Yes . . . *You can have opportunity, but if their children are left we're gonna have them butchered. We can make a strike but we'll be striking against people that we don't want to strike against. And what we'd like to get is the people who caused this stuff and some, there's some people here are prepared to know how to do that . . . go in town and get Timothy Stoen, but there's no plane, there's no plane, you can't catch a plane in time. He's responsible for it. He brought these people to us. He and Deanna Myrtle. But people in San Francisco will not, not be idle over this. And not take our death in vain, you know . . .*

Interruption

"Yes, Christine..."

—*JIM JONES*

IN THOSE FINAL MOMENTS of death, there was only one person who openly dissented. Christine Miller was known as someone willing to challenge Jim Jones. As everyone offered their final praise of Jones, Miller wanted to know if there were any other options. If there was a saint in those moments, it's Christine Miller. She stood up when nobody else would. Jesus was in her. May he be in us too.

Amen.

Late

"Is it too late for Russia?"

—CHRISTINE MILLER

Regardless of what anyone said, life was still important to Christine Miller. As the only person who pushed back against Jim Jones' rush to mass suicide, Miller deserves our admiration. Grasping for anything that would save lives, she suggested that the entire community go to Russia. Is it too late? Miller asks a question that stirs in all of our souls. When we wonder if it's too late, let us remember that there is no such thing. The hour of grace is always here. In every situation, the choice remains the same . . . either we will speak our truth or it we will die. Like Christine Miller, Jesus spoke a truth that never died. Go and speak likewise.

Amen.

Jim Jones: Here's why it's too late for Russia. They killed. They started to kill. That's why it makes it too late for Russia. Otherwise I'd said, "Russia, you bet your life." But it's too late.

Control

"I can't control these people. They're out there."

—JIM JONES

THROUGH A CONSISTENT USE of fear, Jim Jones pushed the people closer and closer to death. There's never any understanding of who "these people" are. If people can convince you to be afraid of "these people," they will control your life. "These people" are everywhere "out there." Those who feel like they're under imminent dangerous threat will do whatever it takes to avoid that threat. Jones knew this. Ultimately, the community died because of "these people" and "out there." Christine Miller knew better. As Jones spoke, she kept pushing for more truth. There are no lies in Christ Jesus. In the struggle for light, Miller shows us what to do when anyone tries to control us with statements like "these people" or "out there," keep demanding the truth.

Amen.

Jim Jones: They've gone with the guns and it's too late. And once we kill anybody, at least . . . that's the way I've always . . .

Lot

"I've always put my lot with you."

—JIM JONES

THERE IS CHRIST AND there is Anti-Christ. In what might sound like the words of Christ, Jim Jones declared that he was putting his lot with his community. Unfortunately, this didn't turn out to be . Jones was pushing the community to a suicide that he would not fully emulate. When the time came, almost everyone in the community took a lethal dose of cyanide. Afraid of a similar death, Jones was found with a lethal bullet wound in his head. I can't imagine Christ pushing people to a painful suicide and then taking an easier route. When someone tells you they're with you, make sure they mean it. There's nothing worse than finding out that someone is a liar than when your life is on the line.

Amen.

Jim Jones: And when one of my people do something, it's me . . . .
Understand, I don't have to take the blame for this, but I don't live that way. They said deliver up Jjara, who tried to get the man back here. Jjara, whose mother's been lying on him and lying on him and trying to break up this family and they've all agreed to kill us by any means necessary. You think I'm going to deliver them Jjara? Not on your life. No.

Crowd: No! No!

Unidentified Man: Is there any way if I go, that it'll help?

Jim Jones: No, you're not going. You're not going.

Crowd: No! No!

Jim Jones: Not going. I can't live that way. I cannot live that way.

For

"I've lived for all and I've died for all."

—JIM JONES

THESE WORDS SHOULD BE the mantra of our lives. The path of Jesus is about living for all and dying for all. The problem with Jim Jones is that living for all shouldn't include killing all. Jones said these words right before extermination. What if Jones had really meant these words? Can you imagine if Jones had followed the path of Jesus and offered himself as a sacrifice for the betterment of the community? Jones was too scared for that. With his health failing and serious legal issues approaching, Jones was ready to commit suicide . . . he just didn't want to do it alone. There is no sacrifice here. There is only cowardice. As time ran out, Jones' words were proven void. Jones didn't live for all. Jones didn't die for all. Like at every other moment of his life, Jones was going to take care of himself. Surely, we can live differently?

Amen.

Crowd: Applause

Hope

"I've been living on a hope for a long time, . . ."

—*JIM JONES*

HOPE IS NOT ALL that complicated of a construct. When we find it, we're alive. When we don't, we're dead. There is no life apart from hope. Hope is God. God is Hope. When I hear Jim Jones' words, I struggle to believe him. I know what was about to happen and so did he. Hope is about life not death. A synonym exposes the lie, "I've been living on a God for a long time . . ." Jones hadn't been living "on a God" for a very long time . . . if at all. In the midst of the deceit, it's important to remember that the lies of the speaker cannot destroy the possible truth of their words. "I've been living on a hope for a long time . . ."

Amen.

Jim Jones: Christine, and I appreciate–

Agitation

"You've always been a very good agitator. I like agitation because you have to see two sides of one issue..."

—JIM JONES

People consistently talk about their love for agitators... as they express their hate for agitation. For Jim Jones, there wasn't ever two sides to any issue. There was only one side, his. In this context, it seems like Jones is simply trying to manipulate Christine Miller in their final exchange. He compliments her in order to kill her. Can you imagine how many people complimented Jesus? Where were they in the end? Why didn't they try to save his life? Beware of compliments... sometimes they're lethal.

Amen.

Jim Jones: . . . two sides of the question. What's those people gonna get done once they get through?

Hell

"They make our life worse than hell..."

—JIM JONES

PARANOIA ENGULFED JIM JONES. Enemies were everywhere. Jones acted increasingly irrationally. I'm not sure that you can say that their enemies made their life worse than hell. I think it would be more accurate to say that Jones made their life worse than hell. The evil was always within. Before you start blaming your enemies for your hell, make sure you're sure that you don't need to blame yourself.

Amen.

Jim Jones: . . . , they'll make the Russians not accept us. When they get through lying . . . They told so many lies between there and that truck that we are, we are done in as far as any other alternative.

Christine Miller: Well, I say let's make an airlift to Russia, that's what I say.

Belief

"I don't think nothing is impossible, if you believe it."

—CHRISTINE MILLER

IN A VERY PUBLIC final engagement with Jim Jones, Christine Miller tried to save Jonestown. Miller's words were words of tremendous beauty. She believed that hope could hold back evil. The community wasn't having it. Eventually, Jones and the others cut her off. Many would say that failed. Everybody did still die. I think it's unfair to judge Miller in such a way. Her words should be judged in context. As death approached, Miller's hope was the last hopeful words many would ever hear. The words followed the listeners to eternity . . . for hope is always immortal.

Amen.

Jim Jones: But how we gonna air . . . How' re you going to airlift to Russia?

Christine Miller: Why, I thought they said if we got in an emergency, they gave you a code to let them know.

Jim Jones: No, they didn't. They gave us the code that they'd let us know of an issue, not us create an issue for them. They said if we . . . if they saw the country coming down, they'd agreed they'd give us the code, they'd give us a code. You can check on there and see if it's on the code. Check with Russia to see if they'll take us in immediately. Otherwise we die. I don't know what else you say to these people. But to me death is not . . .

Fearful

"... *death is not a fearful thing* ..."

—JIM JONES

REPEATEDLY, JIM JONES USED the promises of God to manipulate his followers. Though God tells us to never fear death, God didn't tell us to chase it. Jones said these words a short time before everyone died. These moments were not about God. These moments were about the false divinity of Jones. People shouldn't have feared death . . . Jones was the one they should have feared. Quietly, I'm sure they did.

Amen.

Jim Jones: . . . , it's living that's treacherous . . .

Crowd: Applause

Never

"I have never, never, never, never seen anything like this before in my life."

-JIM JONES

WHILE I'M SURE THAT Jim Jones had never experienced such pressure, I'm also sure that he brought it all on himself. Whether due to his declining mental health or the evil in his heart or some combination of both, Jones repeatedly inflicted violence on people. Justice was getting very close. Instead of defending himself, Jones quit. After the gunshot, Jones' soul departed his body. In the absence of answers, we're left to wonder what it feels like to know your lies brought about a massacre. When Jones met God, I'm sure he quickly learned how to tell the truth.

Amen.

Jim Jones: I've never seen people take the law . . . and do . . . in their own hands, and provoke us and try to purposely agitate and murder of children.

Worth

"There's no use, Christine, it's just not worth living like this..."

—JIM JONES

Is LIFE WORTH LIVING? The question is one of survival. Jim Jones was ready to quit. Obviously, Christine Miller thought differently. As she surveyed the scene, Miller believed life was worth it. Eventually, death shouted her down. For the gathered, they'd become convinced that life was dead. They were ready for it all to end. The rush to death was a rush to deny life. God gives us life so that we might give others life. The message of Jonestown is that death leads to death.

Amen.

Jim Jones: . . . not worth living like this.

Similar

"I think that there were too few who left for twelve hundred people to give them their lives, for those people that left."

—CHRISTINE MILLER

JUST A FEW HOURS after a small group defected from Jonestown, Christine Miller tried to convince Jim Jones that these defectors were no reason for everyone to die. Jones disagreed. In the midst of Jones' supreme authority, Miller was desperate for a way out. There was no way out. Armed guards surrounded the camp. Death was no longer a choice. Everyone was going to die. Sometimes, I think that our relationship with God is like this. God is armed and there is no way out alive. Death is coming. Is our spirituality similar to those final moments in Jonestown? God, I hope not.

Amen.

Jim Jones: Do you know how many left?

Christine Miller: Oooh, twenty odd . . . that's, that's small . . .

Jim Jones: . . . twenty-odd, twenty-odd . . .

Christine Miller: Compared to what's here.

Jim Jones: . . . twenty-odd. But what's gonna happen when they don't leave. I hope that they could leave . . . but what's gonna happen when they don't leave?

Christine Miller: You mean the people here?

Jim Jones: Yeah, what's gonna happen to us when they don't leave? When they get on the plane and the plane goes down?

Christine Miller: I don't think it'll go down.

Jim Jones: You don't think it'll go down?

Crowd: Yes it will . . .

Jim Jones: I wish I could tell you you were right, but I'm right. There's one man there, who blames, and rightfully so, Eddie Blakey, for the murder, for the murder of his mother and he'll sh . . . he'll stop that pilot by any means necessary.

Fly

"He'll do it. That plane will come out of the air. There's no way you can fly a plane without a pilot."

—JIM JONES

JIM JONES REVEALED HIS involvement in the plot to murder the delegation that'd just left Jonestown. Jones' henchman reached the runway as the delegation was boarding their planes and opened fire. This action preempted the original plan to have a false defector shoot the pilot in midair. Congressman Leo Ryan, several reporters and a defector were murdered and numerous others were injured. Paranoia led to murder and would again. Jones praised the poison. Trusted lieutenants handed it out. Jones didn't kill alone. There were copilots. If there hadn't been, the massacre would have never happened. The tragedy occurred because of the orders of the pilots. There is a tremendously spiritual lesson to be learned in all of this . . . be careful who you fly with.

Amen.

Christine Miller: I wasn't speaking about that plane. I was speaking about the plane for us to go to Russia.

Jim Jones: How do . . . To Russia? Do you think Russia's gonna want . . . no they're not gonna . . . Do you think Russia's gonna want us with all this stigma?

Value

"We had really had some value ... but now we don't have any value."
—JIM JONES

WHEN PEOPLE DECIDE THEY'RE worthless they're incredibly dangerous to themselves and everyone around them. There is truly nothing more frightening than people who have nothing to lose. After the shooting of the delegation, Jones believed the community had nothing else to live for. Convinced that their worth was in the past, Jones and his leadership became more and more dangerous. Ultimately, the massacre was realized. The problem with Jonestown was their value centered on one man. Worth comes from something much bigger than that ... God.

Amen.

Christine Miller: Well, I don't see it like that. I mean, I feel like . . .

Hope

"..as long as there's life, there's hope."

—CHRISTINE MILLER

CHRISTINE MILLER BELIEVED IN hope. Jim Jones killed hope. Occasionally hope and death go together. That wasn't the case in Jonestown. Jesus died to give hope to the cosmos. Who was Jones trying to share hope with? After the people of Jonestown arrived with such great expectations, Jones slowly killed them. In those final moments, Miller grasped for hope. There was none to be found. By the time the massacre arrived, life was gone and hope was dead. The bodies dropped soon thereafter.

Amen.

Christine Miller: That's my faith.

Someday

"Well, someday we're gonna die, someplace that hope runs out."

—JIM JONES

PASTORS SHOULD CULTIVATE HOPE. Jim Jones cultivated hopelessness. Thankfully, there is a real hope that can be hopeless. God is in us. As the years progressed, Jones might have left God but God never left him. God can't leave us. God is in us. God is hope. After Jones breathed those final breaths, he met hope face to face.

Amen.

Jim Jones: . . . 'cause everybody dies.

Crowd: Right, right.

Choose

"I haven't seen anybody yet that didn't die. And I'd like to choose my own kind of death for a change."

—JIM JONES

ON HIS FIRST POINT, Jim Jones was right. Death is coming. Those who expect death are often the ones who live life most fully. Jesus knew death was coming. Life came from life. In the midst of Jonestown, Jones didn't care about such concepts. It was murder time. Manipulation was the lethal weapon. There is nothing moral about such a situation. In those final moments, evil reigned. To work for death is to deny the image of God. When life was the answer . . . Jones chose death.

Amen.

Tired

"I'm tired of being tormented to hell..."

—JIM JONES

WITHOUT QUESTION, JIM JONES was very sick. Sometimes, sick people want everyone to feel their pain. Selfishness leads to warped thinking. Jones didn't want to die alone and decided to take Jonestown with him. This contrasts starkly with the actions of Jesus. Every step of the way, Jesus sought to sacrifice his life. Jones sacrificed his life for no one. Quite simply, Jones led hundreds to their death because he was scared. Contrary to his statements, Jones' actions had nothing to do with Jesus. The only thing Jones had to do with was Jones. Hell is being selfish until the very end.

Amen.

Jim Jones: . . . that's what I'm tired of.

Crowd: Right, right.

Jones: Tired of it.

Applauding

"Applause"

—CROWD

PEOPLE APPLAUD THEIR OWN demise. Why? Perhaps, it's a tactic to distract the mind from what's coming. Don't get me wrong . . . there were pure believers in Jonestown. Those folks applauded out of joy. However, not everyone shared the joy. In the midst of certain doom, many people applauded because they didn't know what else to do. The problem is that the applause masked any dissent. Everyone simply applauded themselves to death. There was one who put her hands down and stood up, Christine Miller. Unfortunately, no one joined her. Everyone wanted to keep applauding. The applause was a mistake with great consequences. Be careful . . . applause can be deadly.

Amen.

Jim Jones: Tired of people's lives in my hands and I certainly don't want your life in my hands and . . .

Meaning

"I'm going to tell you, Christine, without me, life has no meaning..."
—JIM JONES

As I stood by his hospital bedside, he told me what happened. After he described the beating, I asked him tell me how he felt. I was very concerned. After a moment, the man replied, "My partner has always told me that my life would have no meaning without him... I believe him." Though deeply concerned, I decided to just listen. After years of repeated incidents, the partner was arrested after a brutal beating. When I went to visit the hospital, the man strained, "I'm brainwashed. Help me get away from him." After some hard work, he escaped. The people of Jonestown weren't so lucky. Jim Jones told the people that their lives would have no meaning without him. Since there was no one there to contradict, everyone simply believed Jones. Professing love, Jones repeatedly abused the people of Jonestown. The love turned out to be a lie. Abuse is often appears disguised as love. Be careful.

Amen.

Friend

"I'm the best friend you'll ever have."

—JIM JONES

FOR MANY YEARS, I didn't have a ton of friends. So, my only friend was a very important friend. I suspect my friend knew that I needed a friend. It probably wasn't difficult to see. Over time, my friend became less of a friend and more of an abuser. From jokes to lies to hits to other attacks, I felt like less and less of a human. I didn't know what to do. I was trapped. Through it all, I remember the abuser repeating, "I'm the best friend you'll ever have." For a long time, I believed him.

Jim Jones was no dummy. Recognizing the immediate power of placing himself as the best thing that would ever happen to the community, Jones used the phrase to kill. When you hear the words, "I'm the best friend you'll ever have," you're hearing the devil. The only way to beat back the devil is to say with deep conviction, "No . . . you are not."

Amen.

Jim Jones: And once, once I have to pay, I'm standing with Jjara, I'm standing with those people. They're part of me. I could detach myself . . . my attorney says detach myself . . . no, no, no, no, no . . .

Troubles

"I'd never detach myself from any of your troubles. I've always taken your troubles right on my shoulders and I'm not gonna change that now."

—JIM JONES

"I KNOW HOW YOU feel." Have you ever heard that phrase before? I hate it. How can you know how I feel? Such an understanding is impossible. You can't feel how I feel. To say that you know how I feel is to lie. When you lie, your credibility is slowly depleted. By the end, Jim Jones should have had no credibility left.

By claiming to be so closely bound to the troubles of each member of the community, Jones performed loyalty. It was never real. Even if he had really wanted to, it would have been impossible for Jones to carry everyone's burdens. That's just not the way it works. Jones performs loyalty in order to divinize his person. If Jones had been able to carry the troubles of the community, why didn't he take them away? Because . . . he didn't know them. He only knew his. When one concentrates only on the self . . . death comes quickly.

Amen.

Late

"It's too late. I've been running too long. Not gonna change now..."
—JIM JONES

I'VE HEARD TALK LIKE this many times before. "I can't change." "I'm set in my ways." "It's don't know how to live differently." Such talk means, "I don't want to change." or "I don't want to grow." Jesus never stops changing. Jesus never stops growing. Change is synonymous with Jesus. Since Jesus is changing with and in us, Jesus is the same change yesterday, today and forever. Despite his claims to the contrary, Jim Jones was obviously not Jesus. Interested in manipulating the community, Jones didn't want to change because he was ready to die and wanted to take the community with him. Be careful of those who resist change, they're the biggest threat to your future.

Amen.

Jim Jones: Maybe the next time you'll get to go to Russia . . . the next time 'round . . . This is, what I'm talking about to now is in the dispensation of judgment. This is the revolutionary . . .

Revolution

". . . this is revolutionary suicide . . ."

—JIM JONES

CAN SUICIDE EVER BE revolutionary? Many have given their lives in revolutionary ways. Jesus comes to mind. So, what is the definition of revolutionary suicide? I suspect that a revolutionary suicide must be revolutionary. I'm not certain that the deaths at Jonestown were revolutionary. There is no way to refer to the children as having committed suicide. The actions taken against them were murder. There were also people who were coerced or forced to commit suicide. I would call such actions murder. So, did the people who committed suicide commit revolutionary suicide? I have no doubt that the people thought they were dying for the revolution. It's so sad they were duped. Jim Jones committed suicide because he was paranoid and dying anyway. I wouldn't necessarily call that revolutionary. Truth be known, I think that Jones knew there was very little revolutionary about their actions. God often calls us to give our lives. Occasionally, suicide can be revolutionary. If you ever thinking about it . . . choose the right revolution.

Amen.

Jim Jones: ... council, I'm not talking about self, self-destruction. I'm talking about what, we have no other road. I will take your call. We will put it to the Russians, and I can tell you the answer now, because ...

Prophet

"... I'm a prophet."

GOD CALLS PROPHETS. THERE are always people set aside to tell the truth. It's not hard to judge Jim Jones' claims to prophecy. You can't be a prophet if you don't tell the truth. When we engage prophets, truth should be our guide . . . just make sure it's true.

Amen.

Jim Jones: Call the Russians and tell them and see if they'll take us.

Afraid

"Not that I'm afraid to die..."

—CHRISTINE MILLER

WHAT'S WRONG WITH FEAR? It's natural. Right? When Jesus was being led to the cross... don't you think he was a little afraid? Jesus knew what was going to happen and still carried fear. Do you think you're better than Jesus? Jim Jones did. After many years of proclaiming his love for Jesus, Jones decided he was Jesus. I feel like those who talk about being fearless are usually the ones who are most afraid. What we vocalize is often an attempt to deflect. Were they afraid to die? Christine Miller said she wasn't. I don't believe her. I think she was just trying to kept it together. I wish more people in Jonestown had been afraid to die. Maybe fear would have saved lives. Unfortunately, the community was so worried about loyalty that fear was secondary. There is nothing wrong with having a fear of death... often it keeps us alive.

Amen.

Jim Jones: I don't think you are . . . .

Christine Miller: By no means . . .

Jim Jones: I don't think you are . . .

Babies

"But I look at all the babies and I think they deserve to live..."
— CHRISTINE MILLER

BABIES ARE HOPE. I will never forget holding each of our first five children. Looking into their eyes, I dreamed. In retrospect, I believe they did the same thing. Christine Miller had a similar experience. She dared to look into the eyes of the babies of Jonestown. There, Miller found hope. As the seconds perished, hope was hard to come by. In the midst of it all, Miller attempted to save their lives. It was not to be. Death had already gained too firm a grip. Jim Jones was too far gone. We are not. Babies can save us. Babies are hope. Don't believe me? Just look to the baby of Bethlehem.

Amen.

Jim Jones: I agree . . .

Christine Miller: You know . . .

Jones: But also they deserve . . .

Peace

"... what's more they deserve peace."

—*JIM JONES*

WAS THERE EVER PEACE in Jonestown? For some, peace might have visited occasionally. But for the most part, the community lived under a constant barrage of abuse. Peace was hard to come by. In the end, Jim Jones promised peace. There was no such thing. In those final moments, Jones talked like peace was synonymous with death. In his argument with Christine Miller, Jones is defended the murder of babies by declaring their need for peace. While it might be true that there is peace in death, there is no peace in murder. Jim Jones and his closest associates murdered baby after baby. There is no peace in such abuse. In death, I believe that God embraced all of those babies with a peace that passes all understanding. There was and is everlasting life for those babies. With such affirmed and sealed for all of eternity, what happened in Jonestown had nothing to do with peace. Jonestown was about terror. Make no mistake, God picked up the pieces of Jonestown and made all things right. In God's love, I believe that peace eventually found them all.

Amen.

We

"We all came here for peace..."

—CHRISTINE MILLER

"THE GRASS ISN'T ALWAYS greener on the other side." I've heard the phrase innumerable times. I never truly knew what it meant until I got a little older. Earlier in life, I fled any time I experienced hardship. When I stopped, I often realized that my new home was just as bad as my old one... if not worse. On at least one occasion, my new home was so bad that I immediately moved. Through it all, I learned the grass was definitely not always greener on the other side. I've often wondered how many people moved to Jonestown with great hope and quickly realized peace was dead. Christine Miller points out her disappointments. Our homes are our futures. Be careful where you live.

Amen.

Jim Jones: And we, have we had it?

Christine Miller and Crowd: No . . .

Jim Jones: I tried to give it to you. I've laid down my life, practically, I've practically died every day to give you peace . . . and you still not have any peace.

Flattery

"You look better than I've seen you in a long while . . ."

—JIM JONES

FLATTERY IS BULLSHIT . . . meaningless words. Jim Jones' words are downright offensive. If someone says you look better now than you did before, what did they think you looked like before? Jones flatters to belittle and control. Can you imagine Jesus saying such things? If Jesus had talked to people like Jones did, he would have turned out like Jones. But, he didn't. His words healed. Jones' words were the words of a predator. The people of Jonestown never had a chance. By the time death arrived, Jones had filled their lives with so many empty words and bullshit promises that most were ready to follow him anywhere. The problem is that flattery only gets you nowhere. If you believe flattering words and base your life on them, such words can get you killed. Regardless of what evil might say, Jesus is ultimate truth and the truth of Jesus is far more transformative than any bullshit a flatterer could ever share.

Amen.

Jim Jones: . . . but it's still not the kind of peace that I want to give you.

Fool

"The person's a fool who continues to say that you're a winner when you're a loser . . ."

—JIM JONES

DO WINNERS AND LOSERS exist? Jim Jones consistently strived to be a winner. Every day, Jones filled his life with people worshipped his assumed wins. Ultimately, such affirmation became his undoing. Labeling people as winners and losers is incredibly problematic. Such rankings are always about power . . . who has it and who doesn't. Jones shamed the people of Jonestown to suicide by telling them that they would be losers if they didn't. They wanted his approval that bad. Death was a chance to prove their love. In retrospect, it is clear that there were no winners or losers in Jonestown . . . there were only victims.

Amen.

Jim Jones: Win one, lose two . . .. What? I didn't hear you, ma'am, you have to speak up . . . That's a sweet thought, who said that? . . . Come on up and speak it again, honey. Stand up and say it about (inaudible) . . . love . . . (inaudible) is taking off, no plane is taking off . . . It's suicide. They have done it . . . Stoen has done it but somebody ought to live . . . somebody . . . can they talk . . .

Infamy

"... *can they not talk to San Francisco to see that (Tim) Stoen does not get by with this infamy, with this infamy? He has done the thing he wanted to do, to have us destroyed."*

—JIM JONES

THE CUSTODY BATTLE BETWEEN Jim Jones and Tim Stoen over John Victor Stoen was the defining conflict in the history of Jonestown. Under pressure, Tim Stoen signed a false affadavit that said Jones was John Victor's father. Joined by John Victor's mom, Stoen fought to regain custody. As negative custody rulings mounted, Jones fled with John Victor to Jonestown. With other concerned people, Stoen publicly fought back. Eventually, Congressman Leo Ryan organized a Jonestown investigative delegation. Ryan and others were murdered. Jones led the remaining community to commit suicide. In his hate, Jones couldn't die without slamming his great troubler. Not long after these words, John Victor Stoen died in Jones' cabin. He was 6.

May we follow the example of Tim Stoen and live to be great troublers of evil.

Amen.

Destruction

"When you, when you, when we destroy ourselves, we're defeated . . . you are saying, 'Let the enemy defeat us.'"

—CHRISTINE MILLER

FOR A COMMUNITY DONE with Jesus, there sure were a ton of references to him in those final moments. Jones is advocating for a position that followers of Jesus know well. You sacrifice yourself in order to defeat the enemy. Christine Miller understands Jones' provocations and argues that you are defeated when you destroy yourself. Whether this is true or not is complicated, certainly there have been instances throughout history where people intentionally destroy themselves in order to save the lives of others. Regardless of one's opinion on sacrificial suicides, it is important to point out that this was no suicide . . . the people of Jonestown were murdered. If not directly at the hands of another, the people were murdered by manipulation and coercion. Furthermore, Jonestown's primary enemy came from within. The same man they revered as their God would became their killer. The God that I know doesn't work like this. While we should cautious of our enemies without, the most dangerous enemy is always within.

Amen.

Jim Jones: Did you see, did you see "I Live to Fight No More Forever"?

Christine Miller: Yes, I saw that.

Jim Jones: Did you not have some sense of pride and victory in that man, that he would not subject himself to the will and whim of people who tell that they are gonna come in whenever they please, push into our house, come when they please, take who they want to, talk to who they want to . . . does this let living . . . that's not living to me. That's not freedom. That's not the kind of freedom I sought.

Christine Miller: But I think where they made their mistake is when they stopped to rest. If they had gone on, they would have made it. But they stopped to rest . . .

Beautiful

"It's over, sister, it's over . . . we've made that day . . . we made a beautiful day and let's make it a beautiful day . . . that's what I say."
—UNIDENTIFIED MAN

JONESTOWN DIDN'T STAY SILENT. Christine Miller was threatening the plan. I think these words from the Unidentified Man are the point of no return. He spoke for most, if not all. It was time. Similar interactions would eventually shut Miller down. The man calls the past beautiful. For who? The community was constantly abused and mistreated. There was even speculation that the community had already killed numerous people. The past wasn't beautiful for everyone. This man just wants to make it another beautiful day. We now know that beauty and evil were one in the same in Jonestown. May we all be suspicious of what we call beautiful. In the beautiful things that draw us most . . . often reside the greatest evils.

Amen.

Down

"We win, we win when we go down."

—*JIM JONES*

THROUGHOUT HIS TIME IN San Francisco, Jim Jones presided over a whole host of social ministries. From drug rehab to food distribution to housing, Jones' reach was impressive. By the time he arrived at Jonestown, he cared about power and nothing else. As Jones' health declined, he wanted the community to decline with him. When they didn't seem to be declining fast enough, Jones decided they should all die together. How does one get from social ministry to mass killing? Definitions are important. So often, words are the difference between life and death. Down is about serving the least of these . . . not yourself. If down had been about the least of these, no one would have died.

Amen.

Jim Jones: Tim Stoen has nobody else to hate . . . He has nobody else to hate. Then he'll destroy himself. I'm speaking here not as the administrator . . .

Incarnate

"I'm speaking as a prophet today . . . I wouldn't sit up in this seat and talk so serious if I did not know what I was talking about."

—JIM JONES

WE LIVE IN AN age of prophets. On every street corner, you find someone claiming a word of prophecy. Everybody wants to touch the future . . . but nobody wants to work for it. There are ways to measure a prophet. I think the best way has to do with social justice. Is the prophet driven by a love for all people or by a love of self? In the end, Jones forgot about all people. Death had already set in. Death was inevitable. Prophets are motivated by love not death. In the end, the prophecy failed.

Amen.

Jim Jones: Is there any way to call back . . . the immense amount of damage that's going to be done?

Separate

"But I cannot separate myself from the pain of my people. And you can't either, Christine, if you stop to think of it. You can't separate yourself. We've walked too long together."

—JIM JONES

JIM JONES REPEATEDLY CLAIMED he was God. I think he missed the mark. God doesn't have to claim to be God. God simply is. Despite his consistent failures, Jones was a good actor. In declaring that he was taking on the pain of his people, Jones tried to convince the people that he was Jesus on the cross. When he talked about walking together, Jones imitated Jesus' commands to follow him. The problem with all of these statements is that Jones rarely acted like Jesus. As far as Jim Jones was concerned, whatever he did was right ... because there was no other God in Jonestown apart from him. Jones' claims to divinity failed when he was unable control himself. Then again, are we sure that God has control?

Amen.

Christine Miller: I know that. But I still think, as an individual, I have a right to . . .

Jim Jones: You do, I'm listening . . .

Christine Miller: I think, what I feel, and I think we all have the right to our own destiny as individuals.

Jim Jones: Right . . .

Choose

"And I think I have the right to choose mine and everybody else has the right to choose theirs."

—CHRISTINE MILLER

INDIVIDUALITY IS THE CORNERSTONE of any relationship with God. We're created in God's image. God is independent. To know God is to be independent. When we allow our independence to be taken from us, we are dead. Jim Jones murdered the individuality of the people of Jonestown long before they physically died. Jones sought to destroy the God in them. Even in the midst of such abuse, God always seemed to be speaking. As Christine Miller rose to speak, God spoke through her. Miller's fierce attempt to assert her individuality brought God back into the space. Miller's efforts are how I know God was there. Though she died with everyone else, I have no question that the divinity in Miller will never die.

Amen.

Jim Jones: Mm-hmm . . .

Christine Miller: You know . . . .

Jim Jones: Mm-hmmm. I'm not criticizing, I'm not governing . . . What's that?

Leave

"She talks like she wants to leave us, well, she can go ahead..."
—UNIDENTIFIED WOMAN

IF YOU CAN GET someone to sincerely believe they're damned if they leave, they will stay. The Unidentified Woman's response to Christine Miller exhibited this principle. The Woman gave voice to the belief that anyone who left Jonestown was damned. Her statement is tantamount to the phrase, "go to hell!" The possibility of damnation was enough to guarantee that Miller was counted amongst the dead. While there is much to learn from this interaction, one thing must remain perfectly clear ... we don't have to stay. God is never going to punish us for leaving. God is where we are. When someone encourages you to go to hell, walk away and say, "I just left."

Amen.

Jim Jones: . . . they're our individual lives, that's what you're saying.

Christine Miller: That's right.

Jim Jones: That's today, that's what twenty people said today with their lives.

Christine Miller: I think that I still have the right to my own opinion.

Jim Jones: I'm not taking it from you. I'm not taking it from you.

Extended

"Christine, you're only standing here because he was here in the first place. So I don't know what you're talking about having an individual life. Your life has been extended to the day that you're standing there because of him."

—UNIDENTIFIED MAN

THE UNIDENTIFIED MAN BELIEVED that Jones sustained Christine Miller's life. When Miller talked about her individuality, the Man rebuked her for rejecting Jones' divinity. There was no individuality . . . there was only Jones. Theology is the start of every massacre. Where your God is there your heart will be also. We all make our Gods. The problem with such constructions is that there is no God but God. If the people of Jonestown hadn't accepted Jones' claims of divinity, they would not have followed him to their deaths. Sometimes we have to reject God to find God. Regardless, I believe God was there and her name wasn't Jim Jones.

Amen.

Jim Jones: Despite this, she has as much right to speak as anybody else, too. What did you say, Louvie (phonetic)?

Regret

"Well, you will regret that this very day if you don't die. You'll regret it if you don't . . . that you don't die. You'll regret it."

—JIM JONES

DEATH WAS A DRUG that day. Jim Jones was the pusher. On one or two occasions, I have been in environments where people are using drugs. It was fascinating to me how hard the users were pushing the drugs on other people. It was as if the user could only be comfortable if they weren't the only one using. Jones acted similarly. He couldn't be comfortable with death unless he convinced everyone to join him. In these final moments, Jones would've said anything. Speaking of regret . . . I wonder how many victims of Jonestown regretted the very day they met Jones inthis final moments? When we accept the provocations of a pusher . . . we're going to regret it . . . if we live to tell about it.

Amen.

Christine Miller: (few words inaudible) . . . A man who saved so many people?

Season

"I saved them, I saved them but I made my example. I made my confession. I made my manifestation and the world was ready ... not ready for me. Paul said, 'I was a man born out of due season.' I've been born out of due season Just like all we are and the best testimony we can make is to leave this God-damn world ..."

—JIM JONES

DELUSIONAL IS AN UNDERSTATEMENT. Jim Jones was totally gone. In the depravity of his mind, Jones actually thought he was saving the community. The problem is that Jones didn't know what salvation was. Salvation is about saving. How many people did Jones save that day? Instead of salvation, Jones was about destruction. The most powerful thing Jones could've done that day is exactly what he didn't do ... dump out the poison. Instead of being the savior, Jones was the poison.

Amen.

Crowd: Cheers

Scared

"She must be scared to die."

—UNIDENTIFIED WOMAN

Bullies are everywhere. The Unidentified Woman's words are representative of typical language of oppression. In belittling Christine Miller, the Woman tries to shut her up. It didn't work. With boldness, Miller kept on talking. We all need such courage. When someone tries to shut you up, be fearless ... speak the truth.

Amen.

Christine Miller: I'm not talking to her. Will you let her or let me talk?

Jim Jones: You talk.

Christine Miller: Would you make her sit down and let me talk while I'm on the floor or let her talk?

Rebuke

"... *proper to tell your leader what to do. It really isn't.*"

—*JIM JONES*

IN REBUKING CHRISTINE MILLER for telling him what to do, Jim Jones begins the process of silencing the last bit of opposition in Jonestown. When you give someone authority in your life, it is difficult to take it back. Before this point, Jones authority over Miller was absolute. Jones is simply acting out the role that Miller gave him. Unlike the many moments before, life and death were now at stake. Jones declared that it was time and he expected Miller to get in line. Be careful . . . authority is a dangerous thing.

Amen.

Jim Jones: I've listened to you. You asked me about Russia. I'm right now making a call to Russia. What more do you suggest? I'm listening to you. If Russia gives me one slight bit of encouragement, I just now instructed her to go there and do that.

Unidentified Woman: You won't do no fuckin' good in Russia, God-damn it . . . (pause).

Unidentified Man: All right, now everybody hold it, we didn't come . . . hold it, hold it, hold it, hold it . . .

Jim Jones: . . . much longer to maintain.

Crowd: That's right.

Burdens

"To lay down your burdens, I'm gonna lay down my burdens, down by the riverside..."

—JIM JONES

TO BRING THE COMMUNITY close, Jim Jones used the familiar words of an old spiritual. Even though they'd heard these words countless times, they sounded different that night. In fact, they sounded like a prelude to death. The words were not abstract on that night. The words were for every listener. The words were about them. Would they lay down their burdens? The problem is that they misinterpreted the song. You are to lay down your burdens ... not your life. When someone cites a spiritual, it's important to make sure they know the song.

Amen.

Jim Jones: . . . should we lay them down here . . . inside of Guyana. What's the difference? No man didn't take our lives, right now, he hadn't taken it, but when they start parachuting out of the air . . .

Shoot

"... they'll shoot some of our innocent babies."

—JIM JONES

THE MURDER OF THE innocents is one of the most shocking moments in all of scripture. King Herod killed every young boy in the vicinity of Bethlehem in an attempt to kill Jesus. It didn't work. Jesus and his family escaped to Egypt. Jim Jones knew that most of the community knew the story and used such knowledge to his advantage. No one wants to stick around for children to be slaughtered. Instead of attempting to flee, the people of Jonestown decided to slaughter them on their own. Unsurprisingly, we also now know that Jones was full of shit. There was no invasion coming. Children are our only hope . . . abusing them in any way destroys the future.

Amen.

Jim Jones: . . . they'll shoot some of our innocent babies. I'm not . . . I don't want to see this, Christine.

Fire

"They gotta shoot me to get through to some of these people."

—JIM JONES

WOULD SOMEONE REALLY GIVE their life for you? Hell, who wants to find out? I know that I wouldn't want to stake my life on such claims. Jim Jones didn't even know what he was talking about. If he was willing to give his life for anyone in that community . . . why didn't he save their lives? Maybe Jones even thought he was willing to give himself, but such thoughts turned out to be illusory. Rather than sacrificing, Jones was about taking . . . lives and everything else he could get his hands on. Those who are willing to give their life for you are sacrificers not takers. In the end, sacrificers don't have to talk about giving their life . . . they just do it.

Amen.

Jim Jones: *I'm not letting it take Jjara. Can you let them take Jjara?*

Crowd: *No-no!*

Christine Miller: *You wanna see John die?*

Jim Jones: *What's that?*

Christine Miller: *You mean you wanna see John, the little one, who's keep–*

Jim Jones: *I want to keep–*

Crowd: *Loud background noises, inaudible*

Jim Jones: *. . . peace, peace, peace, peace, peace, peace, peace.*

Unidentified Woman: *Christine, are you saying that you think he thinks more of them than other children here?*

Jim Jones: John, John . . .

Unidentified Woman: That's what you're saying–

Jim Jones: Do you actually, do you think I would put John's life above others? If I put John's life above others I wouldn't be standing with Ijara. I'd send John out, he could go out on the driveway tonight.

Christine Miller: He's young . . . they're young.

Jim Jones: I know, but he's no different to me than any of these children here. He's just one of my children. I don't prefer one above another. I don't prefer him above Ijara. I can't do that. I can't separate myself from your actions or his actions.

Unidentified Woman: No way.

Jim Jones: If you'd done something wrong, I'd stand with you.

Take

"If they wanted to come and get you they'd have to take me."

—JIM JONES

"They" is a powerful tool. Who are "they?" For Jim Jones, "they" was about control. If the people believed "they" was out there, it would be imperative to unite to resist. Without "they," there wouldn't have been a "we." The entire operation was based on fear. The more fear Jones produced, the more power he gained. "They" was always necessary, because "we" was manufactured. May we never stop working to turn our "they" into "we."

Amen.

Ready

"Well, we're all ready to go."

—UNIDENTIFIED MAN

SILENCING. IT'S A PHENOMENON that occurs when someone silences another through oppression. It's about power. The silencer exercises power to silence the silencee. Excited to die, the Unidentified Man desperately wants to silence Christine Miller. The Man wants Miller to believe that she is the only person in the room with any hesitancy. The Man knows that Miller is the only thing that stands between him and death. In the midst of the conflict, the two were of the same mind on one thing ... they both knew that the quickest way to death was for Miller to stop talking. That's why Miller kept talking. While we don't completely know what happened to Miller, I bet she was never silent. God wasn't either.

Amen.

Unidentified Man: If you tell us we have to give our lives now, we're ready. I'm pretty sure all the rest of sisters and brothers are with me.

Sovereign

"For months I've tried to keep this thing from happening but I now see it's the will . . . it's the will of Sovereign Being that this happened to us."

—JIM JONES

WHEN THE END GETS close, many people begin to realize that they still believe in something. Throughout his ministry, Jim Jones had moved further and further away from God. Throwing Bibles in disgust and claiming atheism as his religion, Jones ran away from God as fast as he could. On a consistent basis, Jones even declared that he was God. Regardless of all of his talk and actions, Jones still took the time to cite a "Sovereign Being" in the end. Why would Jones go against what he taught? Without question, death is a strong evangelizer that can touch even the hardest of hearts. While I don't know how it all goes down as the final moments pass, I do suspect that God gives us a little taste of what we've been missing.

Amen.

Protest

"That we lay down our lives in protest against what's been done. That we lay down our lives to protest in what's being done. The criminality of people, the cruelty of people."

-JIM JONES

IS THERE ANY GREATER calling than giving your life for justice? If there is, I can't name it. What about those who commit suicide in protest? Throughout history, people have intentionally laid down their lives in protest. Most think their death will be widely publicized and lead to sweeping change. Unfortunately, this is not usually the case. Often, the response is to denigrate and dismiss. People don't want to be confronted with such a sacrifice. While I celebrate those intentionally lay down their lives in protest, that's not what happened in Jonestown. Few people laid down their lives in protest. Most were murdered. Jim Jones used his power and influence to perpetuate a massacre. In the end, I don't believe that even Jones committed suicide in protest. I think he committed suicide in fear of living. There is no fear in love. Next time you hear of someone committing suicide in protest, measure their actions by their fearlessness and love . . . just like you would Jesus.

Amen.

White

"Who walked out of here today? Did you notice who walked out? Mostly white people, mostly white people walked."

—JIM JONES

JIM JONES WAS AN early champion of racial justice. From the beginning, Jones' communities had large black populations. Jones' family was the first white family in Indiana to adopt a black child, Jim Jones Jr. As time went on, Jones also became very talented at using race to his benefit. By the time everyone arrived at Jonestown, Jones increased his use of such manipulation. Ultimately, Jones used race to push people to their death. By emphasizing that the defectors were white, Jones offered one more reason to commit suicide... you can't even trust those you thought you could. While I'm sure that Jesus felt the same way, I'm also sure that he didn't have to create reasons to keep going. Jesus gave his life for justice ... he didn't have to use race to manipulate other people to join him. Those who protest by committing suicide do so of their own volition not based on racial manipulations. Conversations about race should be used to pursue justice not injustice.

Amen.

Jim Jones: I'm so grateful for the ones that didn't, those who knew who they are. There's, there's no point, there's no point to this.

Accept

"We are born before our time. They won't accept us."

—JIM JONES

ARE WE EVER BORN before our time? The message of Jesus is that we're to live fiercely in the now. Our present passion is what matters. The acceptance of others is not the judge of our success. We're not born before our time. We are born right on time. To think differently is to waste time.

Amen.

Endangered

"And I don't think we should sit here and take any more time for our children to be endangered, for if they come after our children and we give them our children, then our children will suffer forever."

—JIM JONES

THE QUICKEST WAY TO produce an intense reaction from a parent is to threaten their child. Such fierceness comes from God. When fierceness is absent, we should question if love is absent. There should be no question that the parents of Jonestown loved their children. The love was so that it drove them to kill their children. Occasionally, love causes us to make irrational decisions. I wish that some of the parents had revolted out of love. It was not to be. Though not the one Jim Jones intended, there actually is a lesson from God in these words. The only way we can protect our children is to love them with our brains as much as we do our hearts.

Amen.

Christine Miller: . . . *different right here.*

Jim Jones: I have no quarrel with you coming up, I like you. I personally like you very much.

Hostile

"People get hostile when you try to . . ."

—CHRISTINE MILLER

JIM JONES CUT HER off. The dots represent what she could have said. Instead of hearing her out, spoke for her. Consistently, people in power cut the powerless off and speak for them. Jones' didn't use his ears to listen and perpetuated an old injustice. I wonder what more Miller had to say. Could her words have saved lives? We'll never know. In the midst of much talk, Jesus chose to listen. In the midst of much talk, let us remember that the way we use our ears in the fight for justice is just as important as the way we use our mouth.

Amen.

Jim Jones: Oh well, some people do. But then . . . some people do. Put it that way. I'm not hostile. You had to be honest and you stayed.

Run

"If you'd have wanted to run, you'd have had to run with them because anybody coulda run today, they would have wanted to."

—JIM JONES

ON THE DAY OF death, some of the bravest people in Jonestown were those who defected. Risking their lives to maintain life, they pushed toward freedom. You can't push toward freedom in cowardice. Saving life was a direct rebuke of Jim Jones' fierce push to take it. The run of the defectors was simply an indictment of Jones' evil. If saving life makes you a coward, may we all be counted in that number.

Amen.

Jim Jones: *I know you're not a runner and your life is precious to me. It's as precious as John's. And I don't . . . what I do, I do with weight and justice and judgment. I've weighed it against all evidence.*

All

"And that's all I've got to say."

—CHRISTINE MILLER

Resigned that death was inevitable, Christine Miller finally succumbed to those trying to silence her. In the commencement of evil, the questioner must to be neutralized before the injustice can be unleashed. Jim Jones knew what he was doing. By simply letting her talk herself out, Jones neutralized Miller. I don't blame Miller for giving out. I blame the community for shutting her down. In the end, Miller laid silently in Jonestown with the rest of the community. Everyone wanted silence and that is exactly what they got. Don't ever let yourself be neutralized. Your voice might be all that people have left.

Amen.

Now

"And what comes, folks, what comes now?"

—*JIM JONES*

Death.

Amen.

Unidentified Man (in background): Everybody . . . hold it! Sit down right here . . . (loud background noises, agitated). . . Stay seated . . .

Jim Jones (incoherent sounds): Say peace, say peace, say peace, say peace . . . what comes, don't let .. take Dwyer on down to the middle (?) of the east house. Take Dwyer on down . . .

Please

"Everybody be quiet, please."

—UNIDENTIFIED WOMAN

Nerves were growing. Death was close. In the heaviness of the moment, the Unidentified Woman begged for quiet. Quiet seems violent in such a situation. I wonder how the Woman went? I wonder if she went quietly? When she drank the poison, did she cry out? We will never know. We can only know how we would go. During outbreaks of evil, God gives us mouths to speak. Sometimes quiet is murder.

Amen.

Respect

". . . show you got some respect for our lives."

—UNIDENTIFIED MAN

The Unidentified Man was desperate for respect. The difficulty was that he refused to respect himself. The dichotomy is not unusual. Many people spend their entire lives in such hypocrisy. The people of Jonestown had already given their lives to Jim Jones. How could they then grasp for respect for their individual person? However, just because someone doesn't respect their self doesn't mean they aren't deserving of respect. Though, the lack or self-respect does make it difficult. Certainly, we should do our best to lift all people to the level of respect they deserve. The situation in Jonestown had digressed to the point that there was no one to lift anyone up. All respect was gone. Everyone was dead in their disrespect. Ultimately, it makes sense that everyone died. How could anyone live devoid of respect? Whether he knew it or not, the cries of the Unidentified Man were a last gasp for life. No one could hear his cry. The game was up and disrespect was the killer.

Amen.

Sit

"Let me sit down, sit down, sit down."

—UNIDENTIFIED MAN

OVERWHELMED, THE UNIDENTIFIED MAN is looking for a place to rest for a moment. The situation was spiraling out of control. Everyone accepted that death was coming. Could the massacre have been stopped? Maybe. Could the community have been saved? Possibly. Could death have been turned back? Perhaps. We will never know. The people of Jonestown were too busy sitting down rather than standing up.

Amen.

Jim Jones: I know . . . Mmmm-mmmm-mmm.

Tried

"I tried so very, very hard."

—*JIM JONES*

JESUS DIDN'T TRY. JIM Jones tried. Jim Jones was never able to do. Many people declare that Jones was a monster from the beginning. I can't. There were too many things that Jones did that were very significant. From championing black communities to creating social ministries to fighting for the down and out, Jones was not idle. The problem is that the darker sides of his being always clouded his efforts. Jones got worse as time went on. In some of his final words, I think it is fitting for Jones to say that he tried. Though Jones did many good things, the dark side always got in the way. He never completely made it to do. Jones stayed stuck at try. Jesus tells us how to get to do. We are to give our whole lives completely to our neighbor. Unfortunately, Jones was unable or unwilling and death was the result.

Amen.

Jim Jones: *I've been trying over here to see what can, what can happen (inaudible) who is it–*

(Unintelligible voices)

Jim Jones: *... Get Dwyer out of here before something happens to him ... (pause) ... Dwyer.*

Unidentified Man: *Ijara?*

Jim Jones: *I'm not talking about Ijara, I said Dwyer. Ain't nobody gonna take Ijara, I'm not letting 'em take Ijara ... (pause) ... Gather in, folks, it's easy, its easy. Yes, my love ... (pause)*

Felt

"At one time I felt just like Christine felt. But after today I don't feel anything because the biggest majority of the people that left here were white and I know it really hurt my heart because . . ."

—UNIDENTIFIED WOMAN

THE PEOPLE OF JONESTOWN fled the United States to create a utopian society free of racism. No one realized they'd brought these issues with them. While favoring whites . . . Jones talked about an end to racism. It is fascinating that the people overlooked what was going on right in front of them. While the Unidentified Woman and others talked about the white defectors, she couldn't acknowledge that the leadership assembled in front of her was also all white. While it is important to acknowledge the pain the Unidentified Woman felt, the racists in front of her were not the cure. The people were hopelessly lost in their devotion to Jones. They were convinced that he was the cure to racism and they were prepared to follow him to death. It was the blind leading the blind in those final moments.

Amen.

Broke

"Broke your heart, didn't it?"

—JIM JONES

WHEN EMOTIONS ROSE, JIM Jones always knew how to take advantage of them. Expressed hurts were always Jones' greatest tools to shape the narrative. When you control the narrative, you control the direction. In this moment, Jones took her words and created her death. Fake empathy was the murder weapon in Jonestown. God doesn't have to manufacture empathy. God is empathy. Jones was no God.

Amen.

Heart

"It broke my heart to think that all of these years that the white people have been with us and they're not a part of us. So we might as well end it now because I don't see . . ."

—UNIDENTIFIED WOMAN

RACISM IS HEARTBREAKING. THE evil of prejudice destroys us. However, the defectors didn't because of racism . . . they left to save their lives. It was clear to all who dared to see that Jim Jones was only getting worse. The Unidentified Woman was heartbroken because of racism . . . but I think this was her attempt at a final justification. While I'm sure that racism was a part of everything, the Woman needed an excuse. She knew what she was about to die because she didn't leave. Many black folks defected and survived. To destroy yourself, you have to conjure up justifications. In the end, do you love your neighbor by defecting or staying? I guess there are multiple answers. I think there are many ways to follow the path of Jesus. Maybe many people stayed so that their friends wouldn't have to die alone. When the end came, the Woman died giving her life for her friends.

Amen.

Unidentified Man: Quit talking, the Congressman has been murdered . . . (pause)

Singing and music

Over

"It's all over..."

—UNKNOWN VOICE

SOMETIMES, IT IS OF great benefit to conclude a gathering before significant opposition mounts. Strategically interacting with meetings is about knowing when to keep the conversation going and when to shut it down. The Unknown Voice knew these strategies. By the time the Voice spoke out, any delay was becoming more and more excruciating. By declaring everything over, the Voice was trying to close the meeting and keep the momentum going toward the poison. At this point, the nightmare for many in Jonestown was not to die... but to live. Those who craved death got their wish. The meeting sped up and death reigned. In a very short period of time, it was all over. The facilitators had won. Don't let anyone manage the meeting for you. God created you to make your rules.

Amen.

Jim Jones: It's all over, all over . . .

Legacy

"... what a legacy, what a legacy."

—JIM JONES

WE DON'T GET TO create our legacies. Our legacies create us. Our actions are the tools of interpretation that we leave behind. Jim Jones was so foolish. He was just too narcissistic to get it. He was convinced that he was the only interpreter that mattered. Somehow, Jones believed that hundreds of dead bodies in the jungle of Guyana would be celebrated. Evil is so blind. The legacy of Jonestown is centered on one warning ... we could be next.

Amen.

Jim Jones: But the Red Brigade's the only one that's ever made any sense anyway. They invaded our privacy, they came into our home, they followed us 6,000 miles away. The Red Brigade showed them justice, the Congressman's dead . . .

Medication

"... *please get us some medication. It's simple, it's simple, there's no convulsions with it, it's just simple, just please get it before it's too late.*"

—JIM JONES

I DON'T LIKE MEDICINE. I always worry it's going to make me sicker. Sometimes it does. Regardless, I take medicine because it's possible that it will make me feel better. Jim Jones calls poison . . . medicine. I'm not so far removed from the struggles of this life to fail to understand why someone would want to end their life. I also understand how someone could call the tools of suicide their medicine. The problem with this situation is that the people aren't being given the time to consider the medicine. Jones is rushing everyone toward the poison. Instead of the tools of suicide, they met the tools of murder. In the midst of such moments in our own lives, God whispers, "Be careful of the medicine you take . . . it just might kill you."

Amen.

Jim Jones: The GDF will be here. I tell you get moving, get moving, get moving . . . (unintelligible words)

Voice in background: No, no, no, no . . .

Afraid

"Don't be afraid to die..."

—JIM JONES

THIS IS A PHRASE that both Jim Jones and God are both fond of. Throughout church teachings, we're taught that fear is the antithesis of love. The problem is that Jones' words were not shared in love. Jones wanted to kill. Jones knew that fear was the only thing slowing him down. Even though Jones intended his words for evil, I think God also used them for good. The people needed to know that no matter what happened . . . God would be there. I think many did. There is no fear in love. In the end, there is only God . . . there is only love. So, did banishing of fear kill or heal? If the dead of Jonestown could be raised, I think it'd depend on who you asked.

Amen.

Jim Jones: (unintelligible words) . . . if these people land out here, they'll torture some of our children here. They'll torture our people, they'll torture our seniors. We cannot have this.

Crowd: Right, right.

Jim Jones: Are you gonna separate yourself from whoever shot the Congressman? I don't know who shot him . . .

Crowd: No, no, no, hell no.

Jim Jones: Speak your piece and those had a right to go and they had a right to . . . how many are dead? Oh, God almighty, God almighty . . . Mmmm ? . . .

Unidentified Man: Patty Parks is dead.

Jim Jones: Patty Parks is dead?

Unidentified Woman: . . . you and the others to endure long enough in a safe place, to write about the goodness of Jim Jones . . .

Jim Jones: I don't know how in the world they're ever gonna write about us. It's just too late, it's too late. The congress is dead, the congress lays dead, many of our traitors are dead, they're all laying out there dead. Mmmm? . . .

Good

"Good, good."

—CROWD

EARLIER IN THE DAY, Jim Jones had ordered the murder of multiple members of a delegation that had just visited Jonestown. When Jones told the community that the operation was successful, they paused and declared it "good." Basking in their approval, Jones prepared to kill again. As the darkness of murder descended, God desperately tried to reason with Jones. It was of no use . . . Jones had killed God a long time ago.

Amen.

Jim Jones: I didn't but, but my people did. My people did. They're my people . . .

Crowd: Right, right.

Provoked

"... and they've been provoked too much..."

—JIM JONES

DOES PROVOCATION GRANT SOMEONE a license to kill? God gets provoked everyday. Can you imagine if God killed all the provokers of the divine? The message of God is to love our enemies. The message of Jim Jones is to kill your enemies and then kill yourself. We lose who we are when we allow the provocations of someone else to define us. We kill ourselves every time we respond. There is a better way to live. Remain calm and love on.

Amen.

Crowd: Right, right.

Jim Jones: . . . They've been provoked too much. What's happened here's been too . . . it's been an act of provocation . . .

Blame

"They did it themselves . . . they did . . ."

—UNIDENTIFIED WOMAN

Throughout history, humans have consistently blamed other people for their bad choices. Blame becomes the primary weapon to deflect any personal responsibility. The Unidentified Woman was sprinting toward death and the only words she could muster were an attempt at deflection. Jim Jones was all about the outside threat. In the midst of constant outside blame, the people of Jonestown never took the time to look inside. For that mistake, they paid with their lives. Those who constantly look outside for the source of their problems never realize they are actually rotting from the inside.

Amen.

Christine Miller: *If it's anyways possible to have them to give Ted something to take him, I'm satisfied. O.K.?*

Jim Jones: *What's that?*

Christine Miller: *I said, if it's any way you can do, if you can have them to give Ted something so that he won't have to let him go, too, O.K.? And I'm satisfied.*

Jim Jones: *Yes, that's fine . . . Ted, yes, yes, yes . . .*

Christine Miller: *'Cause I said I never wanted to him to die . . .*

Appreciation

"... *and I appreciate you for everything.*"

—CHRISTINE MILLER

Evil is never the entire story. God is far more complex than that. Even in the midst of the most heinous evil, love survives. In the midst of unspeakable atrocities, there is still something pulling at the soul. Evil cannot live forever. Even though Jim Jones seemed to grow darker by the day, there was a remnant of something left within him ... a remnant of love. Like Christine Miller, the people of Jonestown attached to the remnant and allowed the remnant to define the whole. There is something quite beautiful about finding a remnant in someone. We discover that nothing is as clear as it seems.

Amen.

Only

"You are, you are the only, you're the only and I appreciate..."
—UNIDENTIFIED WOMAN

JIM JONES WAS NOT God. Most of the time, Jones acted as if he hated God. The people of Jonestown didn't care. In their desperation to know God, they created God. The words of the Unidentified Woman were meant for God. The problem was that they were directed at Jones. Praises offered to a manufactured God are deadly... for a manufactured God can never raise us to life.

Amen.

Jim Jones: (unintelligible)

Hasten

"*Please, please. Can we hasten, can we hasten with that medication.*"

—JIM JONES

TIME WAS RUNNING OUT. If Jim Jones still had any piece of a soul left, I would imagine that his guilt was growing by the second. As person after person praised him and said their goodbyes, Jones didn't listen and simply wanted to be done with it all. Even in death, his narcissism was apparent. Death couldn't come quickly enough. There is good reason for Jones to have such feelings. The quicker death arrived . . . the quicker Jones could liberate himself from the guilt. I've often wondered if Jones had any love for the community left. I'm not sure. My suspicions arise from the fact that when you love somebody you listen to what they have to say . . . especially when either party is dying.

Amen.

Jim Jones: *You don't know what you've done . . . (pause) . . . I've tried. (clapping in background) . . . (unintelligible words) . . . They saw it happen and ran in the bush and dropped the machine guns, I never in my life . . . But there'll be more . . . (music and humming in background).*

Move

"You've got to move. Are you gonna get that medication here? You've got to move..."

—JIM JONES

MEDICINE IS POISON AND poison is medicine. Control becomes total when you have the ability to define language. In Jonestown, words were mixed and manipulated with impunity. Such a phenomenon is not limited to Jonestown, everyday I encounter words that don't mean what they are purported to mean. That which is named medicine is often poison. Jim Jones' use of words is not unique. Words continue to oppress. Truth is somewhere else. The only salvation possible is the deconstruction of what we assume is real.

Amen.

Unidentified Woman: Hurry up!

Jim Jones: Marsha, we got 40 minutes.

Unidentified Woman: You have to move and the people that are standing there in the aisle go stand the (unintelligible words), so everybody get behind the table and back this way, O.K.?

Calm

"There's nothing to worry about, so everybody keep calm and try and keep your children calm. And the oldest children can help love the little children and reassure them."

—UNIDENTIFIED WOMAN

OPPRESSION ALWAYS BEGINS WITH six words. "There is nothing to worry about . . ." If you can keep someone from questioning, you can do anything you want. The ushers of death were trying to keep everyone calm. Words did. The people of Jonestown shuffled toward their deaths. The words led them on. Calmly, people killed their children. The words reassured them that everything was going to be ok. Where was a word of life?

Amen.

Crying

"They're not crying from pain."

—UNIDENTIFIED WOMAN

THE MOST PROLIFIC OPPRESSORS are experts at convincing people that what they're seeing is not what they're seeing. The people of Jonestown were being told that the violent deaths they were seeing were actually a peaceful transition. Eyes were confiscated so frequently in Jonestown that nobody could see when the hour of death arrived. When you give away your eyes, you are blind. When Jesus healed the blind, I've long wondered whether it was physical blindness or spiritual blindness. What's the difference?

Amen.

Unidentified Woman: *It's just a little bitter tasting but, they're not crying out of any pain. Annie McGowan, can I please see you back . . .*

Unidentified Man: *. . . have these things to do before I kill you. So let me tell you about it; it might make a lot of you feel a little more comfortable.*

Therapist

"Sit down and be quiet, please. One of the things that I used to do, I used to be a therapist."

—UNIDENTIFIED MAN

WOULD YOU EVER CHOOSE to be operated on by someone who used to be a doctor? The Unidentified Man gave his credentials to grant authority to what he was about to say. The problem was that his credentials weren't current. Wouldn't it be safe to assume that his words weren't going to be current either? Seeing the people of Jonestown as his final patients, the man tried to give comforting words. Despite his pursuit of comfort, his words were nothing but deadly. Would you ever patronize a therapist trying to kill you? God gave you a brain so that you wouldn't have to think about that one too much. Be weary of experts that lead you to death.

Amen.

Unidentified Man: And the kind of therapy that I did had to do with reincarnation and past life situations. And every time anybody had the experience of going into a past life, I was fortunate enough to farther, to be able to let them experience it all the way through their death, so to speak. And everybody was so happy when they made that step to the other side.

Jim Jones: When you accept it . . . you can do but step that way, it's the only way to step.

> *(Sound of babies crying in the background.)*

> *(Music)*

Jim Jones: Be assured in that choice is not ours now. It's out of our hands.

Unidentified Man: Would you have a body that's been crippled, suddenly you have the kind of body that you want to have–

> *(Babies crying in the background)*

Rest

"Calm the children . . . something to give them a little rest, a little rest. Calm the children."

—*VOICES IN THE BACKGROUND*

THE PEOPLE OF JONESTOWN started with the babies first. I guess there was an assumption that it was best to kill the youngest quickly and then move on to the adults. As the children were administered the poison, it became obvious that the poison didn't lead to the quiet peaceful death they were all promised. The entire bodies of the children reacted violently. With loud cries, the children served as a final warning for what was to come. With the knowledge that they could derail the entire massacre, the administrators of the poison wanted the children to be kept calm. It was of no use. The warnings of the children couldn't be contained. There was no rest in the midst of such violence. It is the same now as it was then. Through their deep connection to God, our children warn us of what's to come. They don't need to be calmed. They need to be encouraged. Our lives depend on our ability to listen.

Amen.

Feels

"It feels good, it never felt so good, family, I tell yuh . . . you've never felt so good as how that feels."

—UNIDENTIFIED MAN

WHILE IT'S IMPOSSIBLE TO know for sure, it seems that the Unidentified Man had already drank the poison. In life, you consistently meet poisonous people. Since nobody likes to be poisonous alone, they will do whatever it takes to poison you too. The only defense that you have against the cheerleaders of poison is to fight like hell. Sometimes they force it in you. No matter what happens, may it always be said of us that we refused to pick our poison.

Amen.

(Babies screaming)

Jim Jones: And I do hope that those attorneys will stay where they belong and don't come up here . . . why they did?

Unidentified Man: What happened?

Jim Jones: What is it? . . . Did what? . . . Hard. It's hard, it's hard . . . only first, only at first is it hard. It's hard only at first. Living, you, you're looking at death. It only looks . . . living is much, much more difficult. Raising up every morning, and not knowing what's going to be the night's bringing. It's much more difficult. It's much more difficult.

Crying

"I just want to say something to everyone that I see that is standing around and are crying. This is nothing to cry about."
—UNIDENTIFIED WOMAN

DEATH IS SOMETHING TO cry about. Death was never supposed to be. In the beginning, there was only life. When we cry, we are mourning the loss of life . . . both in the beginning and in the present. The person who looks at death and argues there is nothing to cry about . . . is far removed from a God that joins us in our tears.

Amen.

Unidentified Woman: This is something we should all rejoice about. We can be happy about this. They always told us that we should cry when you're coming into this world, but when we're leaving and we're leaving it peaceful . . . I tell you, you should be happy about this.

Misbelief

"I was just thinking about Jim Jones. He just has suffered and suffered and suffered. He is the only god..."
—UNIDENTIFIED WOMAN

THERE IS NO GOD but God. Though she'd been pushed to believe otherwise, the Unidentified Woman quickly found out that Jim Jones was something else.

Amen.

Unidentified Woman: . . . and he don't even have a chance to enjoy his death here. (clapping and voices in background) . . . I wanted to say one more thing. This is one thing I want to say. That you that've gone and there's many more here. He's still – the way, that's not all of us, that's not all yet. There's just a few that have died. A chance to get . . . to the one that they could tell . . . their lies to. So and I say I'm looking at so many people crying, I wish you would not cry, and just thank Father, just thank him. I tell you about . . . (clapping and shouting) . . . I've been here, uh, one year and nine months and I never felt better in my life. Not in San Francisco, but until I came to Jonestown. I enjoy this life. I had a beautiful life. I don't see nothing that I should be crying about. We should be happy. At least I am. Let's all be the same . . .

(Shouting, clapping and music in background)

Unidentified Woman: . . . Wouldn't be alive today.

Abusive

"I'd just like to thank Dad..."

—UNIDENTIFIED WOMAN

JIM JONES WAS AN abusive parent. Using their love, Jones was able to destroy Jonestown from the inside out. By the time the moment of death arrived, the people were defenseless. Jones controlled their minds. As the poison was poured, people were elated at the chance to die for Jones. Slowly, the poison hit and death set in. They all met someone after they died... by the way... it wasn't Jim Jones.

Amen.

Unidentified Woman: 'cause he was the only one that stood up for me when I needed him and thank you, Dad.

Unidentified Woman: (unintelligible words) and I'm glad you're my brothers and sisters and I'm glad to be here . . . O.K.

Pushing

"Please... for God's sake, let's get on with that we've lived... we've lived as no other people have lived and loved. We've had as much of this world that you're gonna get. Let's just be done with it."

—JIM JONES

WHY WAS JIM JONES in such a hurry? Something gnawed. Something pushed. Something wouldn't let him go. Maybe Jones was battling God? God gnawed. God pushed. God wouldn't let him go. Isn't it interesting that Jones uses the name of God when he believed that he was God. In the end, Jones needed to leave. While his reasons for leaving must have varied, God seemed to be in the mix. Remembering the God he had intermittently known, Jones seems ready to see what's real. Though curious about what was next, Jones didn't want to go alone. Using his control, Jones assured them that there was nothing better than what they'd already experienced. The truth is that... Jones had grown tired of being their God. The weight of the universe is too much for one to take on. Jones believed the salvation of Jonestown was to be found in death.

Amen.

Jim Jones: Let's be done with the agony of it . . . (clapping and shouting in the background). It's far, far harder to have to watch you every day die slowly and from the time you were a child to the time you get gray you're dying . . . . dishonest and I'm sure that they'll pay for it, they'll pay for it.

Revolutionary

"This is a revolutionary suicide. This is not a self-destructive suicide."

—JIM JONES

SUICIDE IS ALWAYS A revolutionary. There is no more discordant of an action than to end your own life. Suicide goes against the natural instinct of preservation. With such affirmed, just because something is revolutionary doesn't make it virtuous. The people of Jonestown were forced into a death that achieved very little for anyone. While I'm not convinced that achievement is the best measure of virtue, I do know that there is nothing virtuous about a forced suicide or murder. While the idea of revolutionary suicide can certainly be applied to many courageous suicides, it doesn't apply here. Jones controlled the minds of his followers. Jonestown was a mass murder. Giving your life for God is revolutionary . . . murder is not.

Amen.

Pay

"So they'll pay for this. They brought this upon us and they'll pay for that. I leave that destiny to them."

—JIM JONES

THOUGH PARANOIA RAN WILD in Jonestown, there is no doubt that the community had real enemies. For years, Jim Jones had destroyed people's lives. The goes around had now come around. An organized and increasingly influential group of defectors and family wanted were desperate to shut the entire operation down and rescue those they love. Under siege, Jones acted to permanently keep the entire community together in the only way he knew how ... by making sure no one survived the night. Even though he was having his way with the community, Jones still clung to vengeance. There is no God in such thoughts. There is only death. When you choose to hate the rescuer and decide to drown, it's a waste of breath to curse them as you go down.

Amen.

(Children crying in background)

Humane

"... who wants to go with their child has a right to go with their child. I think it's humane."

—JIM JONES

HUNDREDS OF CHILDREN WERE slaughtered in Jonestown. What could ever be humane about that? In the midst of great evil, ethics became confusing. Lives depended on truth somehow breaking in. As time ran out, Jim Jones used false words of altruism as a tool to finish the task. Be on guard. When generous words are being thrown around in the darkness, remember that the truth of the humane is the only thing that will keep you human.

Amen.

Jim Jones: I wanna go . . . I want to see you go, though. They can take me and do with me whatever they want to do. I wanta see you go. I don't wanna see you go through this hell no more. No more, no more, no more.

(Babies crying in background)

Jim Jones: . . . We're trying. If everybody will relax. The best thing you do to relax and you will have no problems.

Relax

"You'll have no problems with this thing if you just relax."

—JIM JONES

WHAT HAPPENS WHEN THINGS worse? What happens when children die? What happens when everything starts to die? What are the consequences of relaxation? The massacre at Jonestown was a result of inaction from relaxed people. There is no virtue to be found in relaxation in the midst of murder. In fact, relaxation is the greatest serial killer to ever exist. How many lives would be saved if we decided to stop relaxing? Jesus was about engaging not relaxing.

Amen.

Unidentified Man: . . . the children here . . . a great deal because of Jim Jones. And, the way the children are, laying dead now, I'd rather see them lay like that than to see them have to die like the Jews did, which was pitiful anyhow.

Dad

"And I'd just like to thank Dad for giving us life and also death..."
—UNIDENTIFIED MAN

WHETHER I LIVE OR whether I die, I will thank God. I don't believe that shit. I follow God because God is the God of life. I thank God for life. In the end, there is no death. There is only life. When we transition, we are journeying from life to life. If someone is exalted as the god of both life and death... they are not God. The one true God... the God beyond God... is the God of life. Jim Jones was the god of death... which of course is no God at all.

Amen.

Unidentified Man: ... *and I appreciate the fact the way our children are going because, like Dad said, when they came in, what they're going to do to our children, they're going to massacre our children. And also the ones they take, captive, they're gonna just let them grow up and be dummies like they want them to be and not grow up to be Socialist like the one and only Jim Jones. So I'd like to thank Dad for the opportunity for letting Jonestown be, not what it could be, but what Jonestown is. Thank you, Dad.*

Crowd: Clapping

Friend

"It's not to be feared. It is not to be feared. It's a friend, it's a friend."

—JIM JONES

WHILE I CERTAINLY DON'T believe in fearing death, I don't trust the person who tells me that death is a friend. I'm afraid they met want to introduce me to their friend. I prefer the ones I've got. Isn't God the only friend we need anyways?

Amen.

Jim Jones: You're sitting there. Show your love for one another . . . (unintelligible words) . . . let's get calm, let's get calm, let's get calm.

(Babies screaming in background)

Jim Jones: . . . to us . . . we had nothing we could do, we can't . . .

Separate

"*... we can't separate ourselves from our own people.*"
—JIM JONES

GOD CANNOT BE SEPARATED from the people of God. God is the bond that unites all communities. God is not relegated to any particular people. God is the all in all.

We cannot be separated from the people of God. We are the bond that unites all communities. We are not relegated to any particular people. We are the all in all.

> God is not about separation.
> We are not about separation.
> God is about unity.
> We are about unity.
> God is about love.
> We are about love.
> Seperation is destroyed.

Truth was blurred.

Amen.

Jim Jones: ... pause, children crying in background) ... For twenty years laying in some old rotten nursing home ... (pause) ... taken us through all these anguished years. They took us and put us in chains and that's nothing.... (stuttering) ... there's no comparison to that, to this. They've robbed us of our land, and they've taken us and driven us until we tried to find ourselves ... we tried to find a new beginning, but it's too late. You can't separate yourself from your brother and your sister. No way I'm gonna do it. I refuse. I don't know who fired the shot, I don't know who killed the Congressman. But as far as I'm concerned, I killed him. You understand what I'm saying? I killed him. He had no business coming. I told him not to come.... (long pause) ...

Dignity

"... die with respect, die with a degree of dignity. Lay down your life with dignity. Don't lay down with tears and agony."

—JIM JONES

IN THE BEGINNING, JIM Jones wanted control and got it. Things were different now. With each drop of a body, the community grew less and less manageable. Certain death seems to have a way of lowering inhibitions. In Jonestown, emotions should have been natural. Jones didn't care. Control mattered more than life. God would be exactly what Jones said God would be. In the end, God died. The emotions still lived.

Amen.

Jim Jones: *It's nothing to death, just like Max said. It's just stepping over into another plane. Don't, don't be this way. Stop this hysterics . . . This is not the way for people who are socialistic Communists to die . . . no way for us to die. We must die with some dignity . . .*

Unidentified Man: *That's right . . . . (pause)*

Jim Jones: *. . . soon we'll have no choice. Now we have some choice. You think they're gonna send, allow this to be done and allow us to get by with this . . . you must be insane . . . But children, it's just something to put you to rest . . . Oh, God . . .*

(Babies crying in background)

Mother

"... mother, mother, mother, mother, mother, please, mother, please, please, please, don't, don't do this, don't do this ... lay down your life with your child, but don't do this ..."

—JIM JONES

Is GOD A MAN? Hell, no. So, why do we always assume that God is a HE? We're lost. One of the greatest heresies ever produced is that God is a man. Jim Jones perpetuated such foolishness. However, we can never push God out. God was there. In the midst of the terror, a mother seeks to stop the killing of her child. Though we don't know the details, it's not hard to imagine God in the mix. Can you see her? There is a child being led to death. The child's mother ... God ... springs into action. Diving, God places her body on top of the child. The execution didn't stop. Rather, the child just didn't die alone.

Amen.

Unidentified Woman: . . . *doing all of this for you* . . .

Free

"Free at last."

—JIM JONES

FROM THE PLACE OF arrest to the place of execution, Jesus was pushed. In those final seconds, Jesus experienced tremendous pain. The people of Jonestown were no different. From the place of first manipulation to the place of execution, the people of Jonestown were pushed. In their final seconds, the people of Jonestown experienced tremendous pain. While there is always freedom found in death, it doesn't mean that the death was free... or even necessary.

Amen.

Crowd: Clapping

Quiet

"... *children, it will not hurt if you will be, if you'll be quiet, if you'll be quiet.*"

—JIM JONES

SILENCE IS NOT THE miraculous ointment that cures all pain. The truth is far darker. Silence kills. By promising that silence would erase the pain, Jim Jones killed everyone. What would have happened if people had simply rejected silence? Life would've returned. God is not silent.

Amen.

(Children crying in background, humming, music, pause)

Annihilation

"It's never been done before you say? It's been done by every tribe in history, every tribe facing annihilation."

—JIM JONES

HISTORY DOES NOT CREATE righteousness. Just because something has been done before does not mean that it should be done again. Repetition does not equal morality. The people of Jonestown were restless. What community that is about to be massacred wouldn't be? Dying wasn't as glamorous as Jones had made it out to be. In order to keep the wheels of death going, Jones made an appeal to history. What Jones didn't say was that they weren't the ones facing annihilation . . . he was. History was used as a weapon and it killed more than a few people. Knowing the past is necessary. Sometimes, it's our only defense. Beware of those who make constant appeals to history or you might become history sooner than you anticipated.

Amen.

Jim Jones: All the Indians in the Amazon are doing it now. They refuse to bring any babies into the world. They kill every child that comes into the world, because they don't want to live in this kind of a world. So be patient, be patient . . . death is . . . I tell you I don't care how many screams you hear, I don't care how many anguished cries . . . death is a million times preferable to ten more days of this life. If you knew what was ahead of you, if you knew what was ahead of you, you'd be glad to be stepping over tonight. Death, death, death is common to people . . . and the Eskimos, they take death in their stride. Let's, let's be dignified. If you'll quit telling them they're dying, if you adults will stop some of this nonsense . . . Adults, adults, adults, I call on you to stop this nonsense. I call on you to quit exciting your children when all they're doing is going to a quiet rest. I call on you to stop this now. If you have any respect at all . . . Are we black, proud and Socialist, or what are we? Now stop this nonsense, don't carry this on any more, you're exciting your children.

Crowd: Right, right.

Jim Jones: All over and it's good. No, no sorrow that it's all over. I'm glad it's over . . . Hurry, hurry my children, hurry. All I say, let's not fall in the hands of the enemy. Hurry, my children. Hurry . . . there are seniors out here that I'm concerned about. Hurry, I don't want to leave my seniors to this mess.

Quickly

"Quickly, quickly, quickly, quickly, quickly..."

—JIM JONES

Death was coming quickly. Life was coming quickly. Death was coming. Life was coming. Death was. Life was. Death. Life. Quickly. Quickly.

Amen.

Jim Jones: . . . sisters, good knowing you . . . no more pain now . . . no more pain I said, Al, no more pain. Jim Cobb is laying on the airfield dead at this moment . . .

Crowd: Cheers, shouting and clapping

Jim Jones: . . . remember though this Oliver woman said she, she'd come over and kill me if her son wouldn't have stopped her. These, these are people that are peddlers of hate.

Laying

"All we're doing is laying down our life. We're not letting them take our life. We're laying down our lives..."

—JIM JONES

WHAT DOES IT MEAN to lay down your life? You can't lay down your life unless it's yours to lay down. In the Garden of Gethsemane, Jesus had to make a decision. Am I willing to die so that others might live? Jesus had possession of his life. The choice to die was his and his alone. There was life to give. In Jonestown, nobody owned their life . . . Jim Jones had already taken them all. Death was prescribed not chosen. In the mist of raging injustice, may we always be open to following the path of Jesus . . . and give OUR lives so that others might live.

Amen.

(Background voices)

Jim Jones: . . . not taking their lives.

Want

"We just want peace."

—*JIM JONES*

WHAT IS PEACE? WHO knows? The only thing I know is that it didn't exist in Jonestown.

Amen.

Parents

"All I'd like to say is that my so-called parents are filled with so much hate."

—UNIDENTIFIED MAN

IN JONESTOWN, CHILDREN WERE considered to be children of the community. Every adult was considered a parent. As his children were being slaughtered, the Unidentified Man had the audacity to slam his own parents. If we concentrate too much on others, we will become blind to the hate that is consuming us. God save us from our murdering. God save us from ourselves.

Amen.

Tears

"O.K., stop this, stop this, stop this, children, stop this crying, all of you."

-BACKGROUND VOICE

IN THOSE FINAL MOMENTS, the tears were the last hope. The tears revealed that life still mattered. If people cared, they would try to stop the suicides/murders. Unfortunately, fear killed hope. The people were not alone. As the last bodies dropped, the tears on the face of God dried last.

Amen.

Unidentified Man: . . . in countries. *I think you people out here should think about how your relatives was and be glad about, that the children are being to rest and all I can say is that I thank Dad for making me strong to stand with it all and make me ready for it. Thank you. . . .*

Jim Jones: *All that's, let me –*

Drink

"All they're doing is taking a drink, that takes, to go to sleep . . . That's what death is, sleep . . . . . . I know, but I'm tired of it all."

—JIM JONES

NAMING THE AFTERMATH OF death is a futile exercise. Such descriptions are only speculations. Usually, the person doing the speculating has something to gain from their description. Jim Jones was trying to extinguish every life in the community as quickly and as easily as possible. In the midst of the pain of those final moments, I'm sure sleep sounded very inviting. Just drink. The problem was that everyone saw that it was going to be a nightmare to get there.

Amen.

Loving

"... loving thing we could have ever done, the most loving thing all of us could have done and it's been a pleasure walking with all of you in this revolutionary struggle."

—UNIDENTIFIED WOMAN

IS THERE EVER A time when the most loving thing to do is to kill yourself? While I'm sure that I could think of some scenarios, none of them are remotely close to the evil that played out in Jonestown. I'm not saying there wasn't love there. There was undoubtedly deep love shared between members of the community. No one should ever act as if that wasn't the case. With such affirmed, I don't see how you call this mass suicide/murder loving. The revolutionary struggle is about giving your life to save the lives of others. Who were these folks giving their lives to save? Maybe they thought they were saving each other? Even in the midst of such confusion, God is down with the revolutionary struggle. That's why God keeps dying over and over again.

Amen.

Unidentified Woman: No other way I would rather go than to give my life for Socialism, Communism and I thank Dad very, very much.

Unidentified Woman: That, that Dad's love and mercy, goodness and kindness and bring us to this land of freedom, his love, his mother was the advanced, the advanced guide to Socialism and his love, his mercy will go on forever, unto the . . . (unintelligible word) . . .

Jim Jones: (unintelligible words)

Vat

"Where's the vat, the vat, the vat?"

—*JIM JONES*

POISON. THAT'S ALL JIM Jones cared about. Before the vat, all Jones could think about was doing drugs. Poison. Jones destroyed the lives of so many people. Unable to consider others, all Jones cared about was his self. Poison. Jones convinced God to drink from the vat. Under the pavilion, God drank it fast. Convulsing, God died. Time stood still. Poison. The stuff must not have been that powerful... because God came back. Refusing to stop there, God resurrected all of Jonestown. All was made well. There was something completely new that seemed rather old. Out of the vat, God birthed a revolutionary creation.

Amen.

Jim Jones: Where' a the vat with the green C thing? CN.

On

"Love is to go on . . . (unintelligible words) . . . and thank you, Dad."
                                        -UNIDENTIFIED WOMAN

I DON'T THINK ANYONE knew what God was saying through the Unidentified Woman. In fact, I don't even think she did. If they had, they would have heard these words for what they are . . . fierce words of resistance. These were some of the last words of hope that the people would ever hear. Unfortunately, I don't think most of them could hear. Jones clogged their ears. If they could've heard, maybe their lives would've been saved. Love was breaking into the world to rescue those who were left . . . or maybe love came down to see them through. Listen to the darkness . . . God is still speaking. Can you hear?

Amen.

Jim Jones: The vat, with the green CN please.

Complicit

"Bring it here so the adults can begin..."

—JIM JONES

How can anyone watch children die? The question is not just for the people of Jonestown... the question is also for God. After the birth of Jesus, Herod the Great wanted to make sure that his rule was never challenged. So, he ordered the slaughter of all young male children in the vicinity of Bethlehem. Before the killing began, Jesus and his family escaped to Egypt. As the blood of children ran down the street, God did nothing. When some can save a life and doesn't, they are complicit in the death. God was just as complicit in the massacre at Jonestown. How could there be any difference?

Amen.

Jim Jones: . . . *beg you, don't, don't, fail to follow my advice, you'll be sorry . . . you'll be sorry . . . (unintelligible word) . . . that we'll do it than that they do it.*

(Voices in the background: That's right, that's right.)

Jim Jones: . . . *Must trust, you have to step across . . .*

Sing

"... We used to sing: 'this world, this world's not our home.' Well, it sure isn't...."

—JIM JONES

HOME IS WHERE GOD is and God is our home. If God never leaves us nor forsakes us, how could we assume that anywhere is more home than anywhere else? We are in a constant state of journeying from life to life. Oblivious to God's invitation to be saved from his self-destruction, Jim Jones stubbornly continued in a constant path from death to death. The suicides/killings in Jonestown were not about home... they were about Jones. God was as much home in Jonestown as God was anywhere. Though Jones destroyed their bodies, the people of Jonestown never left their home.

Amen.

Jim Jones: ... We were saying, it sure wasn't ... Really doesn't want, you're telling me. All he's doing is what we'll tell him. Assure these ...

Relaxation

"Can some people assure these children of the relaxation of stepping over to the next plane?"

—JIM JONES

THE CHILDREN KNEW WHAT was going on. God speaks to their hearts and uses their voices. In the final moments of Jonestown, the children were the invitation to salvation . . . the invitation to life. Everyone could have been saved. Unfortunately, the people were too arrogant to hear the children. One by one, they were silencned. People just kept on killing their children and shuffling toward death. From the other side, I can still hear the children speaking . . . don't relax . . . it killed us.

Amen.

Jim Jones: That'd set an example for others. You set 1,000 people who say, "We don't like the way the world is . . . ..

Crowd: That's right, that's right)

Protesting

"... take our life from us, we laid it down, we got tired. We didn't commit suicide. We committed an act of revolutionary suicide protesting the conditions of an inhumane world....."

—JIM JONES

It seems surprising that Jim Jones would waste his last words pushing death. Were there not members of his own family that Jones could have spent his last words on? Couldn't he have spoken about love? What about stopping to reminisce about the beauty of the people in the community? Then again, maybe it's not so surprising that none of these words were shared. From the moment Jones arrived in Jonestown, he wanted death. From conversations to sermons to practices, suicide was championed. Even though Jones talked about the tranquility of suicide, it didn't work out that way. The cyanide is strong. After witnessing the disturbing effects of the poison, Jones decided to shoot himself. Regardless of the form, the result was the same. The vats were half full. Bodies rotted in the grass. Apart from the others, a body lay shot. Flies swarmed the bullet hole. The gun sat dormant. God was dead.

Amen.

(End of Jones talk, music playing, and then silence).

Conclusion

PEOPLE ASSUME THAT GOD forgot about the people of Jonestown. They're wrong. There is nothing that can separate us from the love of God. God was there the entire time. When the people packed up their lives to seek a new world, God was there. When the people took that long boat ride, God was there. When the people arrived, God was there. When life grew difficult, God was there. When the people drank the poison, God was there . . . and God is here. Perhaps, we're the same. We seek a newer world. We long for community. We struggle for love. We're susceptible to evil. It's to easy dismiss the people of Jonestown. It is easy to say that they were out of their minds. Crazy or not, I wish that more people would have the courage and boldness that the people of Jonestown had. In the present, I don't see anyone trying as hard as they did to find a new way. Though Jim Jones ultimately developed into pure evil, I still believe God spoke through him. Throughout the construction of this text, I've seen God use evil to show us the way of righteousness. What better way to know what to do than knowing what not to do? The last words of Jonestown are difficult to engage . . . but aren't the last words of anyone difficult to engage? Is it not human to grasp for some sort of life even in the midst of death? Don't we all want our deaths to mean something?

No one races to die in vain. The people of Jonestown died with great purposed. Theirs was a revolutionary suicide. What can be more revolutionary than to die for love? Though Jim Jones was a powerful manipulator, I'm convinced that he didn't kill over 900 people. Love did. The people were desperate to die together. Love drew them to the poison. Love killed the people. Love is God and God was there. Even in the midst of the horror of it all, the people died for love and those that die for love are martyrs of faith. There is nothing more revolutionary than giving your life for love. How do we become revolutionaries of love? The people of Jonestown know the way.

Amen.

May the God that Has Redeemed and Restored the Slaughtered of Jonestown, Disrupt Your Heart, Mind, Body and Soul . . . As It Was in the Beginning, and Will Forever Be, World Without End. Amen.

The Beginning

www.ingramcontent.com/pod-product-compliance
Lightning Source LLC
Chambersburg PA
CBHW071433150426
43191CB00008B/1113